The Story of Strength

JAIRA B. WILLIAMS

COLLECTION

www.prettyminkdout.com

For permission requests, write to the publisher, addressed "Attention: Permissions Coordinator," at the e-mail address below.

Jaira B. Williams
JairaBWilliams@gmail.com

Ordering Information:
 www.prettyminkdout.com

Special discounts are available on quantity purchases by corporations, associations, and others. For details, contact the publisher at the address above.

Printed in the United States of America

ISBN:978-0-578-53048-2

DEDICATION

This novel is dedicated to ME and all those who have played a significant role in my life. To the struggles, obstacles, and lessons placed alongside the many adversities I've faced, I'm forever thankful. These trials have initiated my purpose and guided me to my TRUTH.

CONTENTS

ACKNOWLEDGMENTS

Jehovah Jireh, my provider. I can't express my gratitude to you enough for the love and favor you have for me. You've shown me who I am and provided me with the necessary resources for your will to be done. You are the teacher, and I am the student. I now know to acknowledge every lesson.

To my parents, the late Sherry & Larry Williams, Thank You for loving me, caring for me, and leaving an unforgettable mark in my life. To be raised by two strong, unique, and firm parents was truly an experience of a lifetime. I've wished often that you were physically here, but I know you've been with me every step of the way. Forever in my heart, I'll love you both eternally.

To my grandmother, Annie B. Epps, you are the foundation of our family. I admire your wisdom, strength, faith, and dedication to Jehovah. Thank you for sewing your seeds into my life. I love you with all of me and more.

To Patrick and Rhonda Grant, Thank You! You both are the epitome of what God Parents truly are. I'm proud to say you have successfully fulfilled your responsibilities by loving, protecting, and guiding me spiritually as your God Child.

To my cousin, Sha Sha, on May 15, 2004, we sat in the hospital room with our family as my mom said her final words to each of us. At the age of 15, her words to you were "Jaira looks up to you. Watch after her." And you've done just that. You always say that you're proud of me, but I'm prouder of you, more than I could ever express. Continue to live out your dreams by expressing yourself freely and being a great entrepreneur, business owner, and the best mom your kids could have.

Reliving my life has been hard enough, so imagine writing a book about it. *The Story of Strength* is the first of many novels to come. To my families, friends, and everyone who has encouraged, motivated and inspired me throughout this process, I appreciate you all and I'm forever thankful, grateful & blessed.

God's Plan

God allowed me to be a character in his story. He outlined my life as I lived the rough draft. He knew with time I would finally come to realize that his plan for me would soon become the story I accepted as My Life. This life was not coincidental. It was awaiting my arrival to finally be published.

He is the author and finisher of our faith.

GENESIS

- *(noun)* - *the origin or mode of formation of something.*

Dear Genesis,

It's me... I know that it has been such a very long time since I've reached out to you. I could say that I've been working and life has just been too busy... but neither of those reasons is good enough for not at least checking in before now.

I heard from Patience that you were still in Tillman. She says you finally took over your mom's old salon. I remember you weren't so interested in hair back in the day. It makes sense though. Hair has been a family business passed on from your grandma to your mom, aunts, and even your cousins. I'd love to come and see the shop again. Are the walls still green? Just thinking about that shop brings back a flood of memories I've all but forgotten. Everything back then was just so simple for us.

It seems like the hardest choice we ever had to make back then was between waffles or pancakes for breakfast. Your dad could whip either up perfect every time. And they weren't complete without a pat of butter carved into a heart on the top. Oh, but then the choice between strawberry jam, maple syrup, apple jelly, or peach preserves... I get hungry just thinking about it.

You had such a great dad in Vaughn. You were the apple of his eye and could do no wrong. When I imagine the type of man I wish I could marry and have be the father of my children, I think about him... I pray for a man like that. I try to be more like Cheryl as I get older. Your mom was always so strong and smart . I can still see her in that hair salon just like it was yesterday. She'd have a line of clients waiting in the front of the shop for everything from a silk press to an outrageous weave. I still remember a lot of her advice to protect my edges and keep my hair moisturized. She used to talk all the time about coming out with her own line of special hair care products. Maybe you can think about doing that now. I am still just so proud I knew such a beautiful, strong, and smart black woman growing up. Watching her just made me feel like I could be and do anything.

I hate to admit to being the jealous type... But I do envy you for the love, warmth and comfort of having it all: a mother and a father living together, under one roof, in a nice house with not one but two nice cars... You all were like the first family of Tillman, GA. People of the community looked up to you all whether on the streets, at school, or church. Looking back, I can see how important it was to your parents to keep you in a protective bubble. I heard the stories growing up, how they lost three little boys. When you came into their lives, you were their little angel. I know that your mom and grandma prayed over you every day.

Genesis, I really am so sorry that it has taken me so long to get in touch with you. Especially under such circumstances. I saw your post online, so I know that you've already heard. I got the news from Faith. I still just can't believe it... I can't believe that one of us is slipping away...

Faith has gone to see her at the hospital in Atlanta. The doctors say that it doesn't look good, so she's preparing herself to receive Miracle's remains. As you know, Miracle really has nobody in this life but us. Fortune has already offered to cover all expenses if she takes a turn for the worse. I'm going to meet her in Atlanta, and we will begin making arrangements with Faith. Did you want to come as well? If not, I understand.

I can't even imagine how hard it's going to be.

Your Friend,

Strength

SERENITY

- *(noun) - the state of being calm, peaceful, and untroubled.*

JAIRA B. WILLIAMS

Chapter One: Daddy's Girl

Serenity Brooks heard the phone in her office ringing as she hurried to her desk, returning five minutes late from her lunch break. She let the phone ring twice more in order to take a steadying breath and look at the caller ID indicating that the call was coming from Holloway Gardens. As the lead Vista Marketing representative, she worked with several departments at Holloway which had an annual calendar booked to the max with seasonal, corporate, and private events. Each event required a sharp attention to detail and that was her specialty.

"Serenity Brooks, Vista Marketing. How may I help you?"

"Serenity, it's Jan ova' at Holloway." Serenity pressed a charmed smile onto her lips as Jan's southern drawl called forth the image of the aging woman's petite frame and out of date, but still adorable, blonde bouffant.

"Yes, Jan. How are you today?" Serenity pushed the long 'A' sound in her words to match that of Jan's honey-dipped southern drawl. It was something she'd learned a long time ago; it's best to pick up the way people that don't look like you speak, especially over the phone.

"Oh, I am wonderful, thank you for asking. I was calling about our seasonal brochures to see when I can come by to pick them up, dear."

"You can come on over anytime you get ready. I've left them just behind the front reception desk in case I'm not in when you come by."

"You are a dream come true, Serenity. I'll be ova' before the end of the day. Thanks again, dear."

"You are very welcome," Serenity assured her before the line went dead. She let out a heavy sigh and reached for the bottle of water at the corner of her desk to rinse away the feel of the fake accent from her throat.

It wasn't long before her phone rang again and she fell into her office mode, handling all calls with ease, even as problems arose or she had to transfer and refer calls to other departments until the cell phone in her pocket buzzed.

"Mr. Hall, it will take me a while to look for that information. Let me call you back."

She cradled her office phone on the receiver as she slid the cell phone from her pocket. Her eyes roamed over the words three times and then over each individual letter and still she was unable to make sense of the message. She looked away from the phone, taking in each individual item on her desk, the computer, the phone, the lamp, the note pad, the desk calendar, and the file tray. It was the real world, her world, but everything felt surreal as she pushed back from her desk and returned her attention and disbelief to the text that just came through from one of her oldest friends.

Her chest squeezed in on itself as she felt a slight shortness of breath. She closed her eyes tight, swallowing hard against a feeling that she was going to lose the contents of her stomach in the next moment. She took three long, slow breaths as she turned her eyes away again from the words that seemed too impossible to be true and forced her stomach to settle down. There were no tears in her eyes, although she was certain that if she were a normal woman there would be. She took in another breath and stood from her chair, counting the steps that it took to get from her office to the bathroom so she wouldn't be able to think about anything else.

She opened the door to the bathroom, closing it behind her before walking to the sink. She wasn't sure what to do with herself now that she was inside. She wasn't going to throw up. She didn't have to use the bathroom. She imagined the luxury of being able to splash water on her face but with the layers of makeup she wore she realized that would make a bigger mess than she was in the mood to clean up. She walked to the mirror, her cell phone still clutched in her hand, displaying the same heart shattering text.

"Miracle slipped into a coma last night..."

Serenity lifted her eyes to the mirror, noticing the lace-front wig that covered her natural hair and the perfect application of foundation and artful contouring of her makeup before she zeroed in to look herself in the eyes. There was no emotion in her eyes, which bothered her more than she thought it would. After all, she'd spent a lifetime hiding her true feelings of vulnerability from everyone. She just hadn't realized that she'd gotten good enough to hide from herself. She rested a hand on the side of the sink, tapping her manicured nails against the porcelain as she tried to decide whether or not she would actually go to the hospital. Of course, her immediate response should be that she would come. But, the thought of laying eyes on her friend's body, which should have been full of life and hope for tomorrow, lying in a coma...

"Why?"

The word came out in a whisper, but still it seemed to Serenity as if it echoed endlessly off the bathroom walls, bouncing against her eardrums in time to the multitude of questions that popped into her mind one after the other. She maintained eye contact with herself in the mirror and marveled at how she could be such an avalanche of tragic emotions on the inside and still look so calm and serene on the outside.

Of all of the people that could and should happen to... why her? Why Miracle?

The door to the bathroom opened, sending an icy chill over the swirling cascade of emotions inside of her, freezing them in place until she could find a more opportune time to examine them. Serenity automatically stood tall, sliding her phone in her pocket before turning on the water to wash her hands. When she finished, she exited the bathroom and went back to her office, closing her door in order to give Strength a call.

"Hey Serenity," Strength's voice was more warm and comforting than she'd anticipated, threatening to thaw the freeze she'd held over her emotions so that she could get through the remainder of her day.

"Hello Strength, I got your text."

"I wasn't sure if I should call or e-mail or..."

"Oh, it's fine. Text is always best if you want me to see something."

"I figured." She could feel Strength's understanding smile through the phone.

"So... what happened?" Serenity heard herself asking, even though she was certain that she was in no way ready for the answer, no matter what had actually happened.

"She had a stroke."

"A what?" Serenity's head began to pound at the absurdity. "She is only... She isn't old enough."

"The doctor believes she may have undiagnosed high blood pressure."

"That still doesn't make any sense. I mean..."

"Her assistant went to check on her when she didn't show up for work and couldn't be reached by phone."

"Shit." Serenity recognized the feeling of grief that began to wrap itself even tighter around her heart. Miracle was always just working way too hard. Why hadn't Serenity insisted that she take it easy, especially after that breakup?

"There is nothing that anyone could have done," Strength said softly.

Serenity was surprised that Strength picked up on how much she needed to hear those words. "Was she... alone?"

"She was alone. But it didn't take even an hour for her assistant to find her."

Serenity was relieved to know this. "You'd think there'd be some kind of sign or warning... you know?"

"I know..."

"I mean... I wish I could remember what the last thing I said to her was. Or even when exactly the last time we talked..."

"You both shared a lifetime of great memories. Don't focus on what you can't remember... Think about what you can."

***

Serenity sat up front in her daddy's pick-up, enjoying the slight bounce of the cabin as the rubbery tires roamed over the uneven pavement of the neighborhood back roads headed towards town. The CD player in the radio finally looped its way back to his favorite track and the usual nostalgic smile touched his lips as he mouthed the beginning lyrics to Stevie Wonder's "Isn't She Lovely."

She turned her head to look at him, giving him a slight smile as it was his special song for her. She still remembered the nights of him putting her to bed and falling asleep to the soft low rumble in his chest as he sang it to her. She hoped that by the end of the song, he'd be in a good enough mood to hear her protest. As the song ended, Serenity jumped on the ten seconds of dead air.

"Why?" She could hear the whining in her own voice and believed that it was just the right pitch to get out of a wasted day at the beauty salon. She looked to her father as the soft smile fell from his mouth and it settled into a firm line of determination. She felt her heart sink a little as she realized there was something different about the stance her father was taking today. She'd gone to church plenty of times with a ponytail and bangs. She didn't see why it was necessary for her to lose a Saturday at home in front of the television for a hair style that wasn't likely to last more than two days.

"Because I said so," he stated as he pulled the car up to Ms. Cheryl's salon.

"I don't want to get my hair done." She tried pitchy whining again. "It takes all day, and I'm tender headed."

"Better a tender head than a tender behind." Her dad gave her a pointed look and she realized that she was on the losing end of the argument and any chance of changing his mind was disappearing fast. Whatever expression crossed her face in acknowledgement of her surrender to having to get her hair done for church made him smile as he extracted his wallet from the glove compartment in front of her and sifted out two twenty-dollar bills. "I want my change back, baby girl."

Serenity took the money and got out of the car.

"I love you," he called after her.

She turned to put her hands on her hips before saying it back. Her dad winked and smiled at her. "I'll be back in a few hours and I really do want my change."

Serenity smirked as he drove away. She walked into the salon, a gust of air blowing in around her as she pushed open the door and swirling with the indoor atmosphere thick with the smell of hot irons, coconut shampoo, and the steady beat of the local radio station playing in the background.

Serenity caught Ms. Cheryl's eye, and she waved her to come sit next to her daughter, Genesis, and another girl she'd only seen around at school. Serenity took the seat on the other side of Genesis, eyeing the new girl curiously as she thumbed at the cash still resting in the palm of her hand.

"Hey Serenity," Genesis greeted her and picked up a magazine from the coffee table in front of them before leaning back in her chair and resting the magazine on her legs. "This is Miracle, she's new in town."

"Yeah, I know. I've seen her at school. Where you from, Miracle?"

"We moved down from Atlanta."

"Your parents moved you from Atlanta to here?"

"Yes," Miracle answered as if this were the millionth time she'd been asked the question.

"So... how do you like it?"

"I haven't really been here for long, but I guess it's okay. I like that I can walk to the movies and the park is nice... not too crowded."

"They don't open up the pool 'til summer vacation," Genesis chimed in. "Once they do, it's off the chain all day every day."

"It sho' is!" Serenity felt herself relax as she lifted her free hand to high-five Genesis. Miracle smiled and then leaned over Genesis' magazine. Serenity shoved her money into her pocket before leaning in as well. Genesis flipped the pages and they sang along with their favorite hip hop and R&B songs that played in the background while waiting to get their hair done.

"Is this my daughter or Beyoncé sitting in my front seat?"

Serenity felt a little shy blush flush her cheeks for the comparison as she got in the truck after her hair was done.

"Whatever Daddy."

"Oh, it's my baby girl. Looking like a young lady. It's First Sunday, Communion tomorrow. You look very pretty. Ms. Cheryl showed you how to wrap that up tonight?"

"Yeah."

"Good. Now, what you want for dinner?"

"Pizza," she answered almost before the question was finished.

"Of course. We'll pick it up on the way home."

Serenity set the table for herself and her dad with plastic plates and cups so they wouldn't have too many dishes to clean that night.

"You finish with your homework?"

"Not yet," she answered as he placed a large slice of pizza on her plate.

"Why not?" he asked with a slightly gruff tone.

"Well," she took a bite of her pizza as she gauged how she should respond. "I was in the beauty salon all day."

"Mmmhmmm..." He poured her a cup of soda before filling his own cup and grabbing a slice of pizza for himself. "Make sure you read your chapter tonight and then study your facts tomorrow."

"Yes, sir."

"You understand that I don't want you to be perfect. I just want you to do your best."

"I understand."

She ate her slice of pizza contentedly before heading to her room to read her history chapter and answer the questions at the end. She took her time wrapping her hair before bed.

She woke up the next morning to the smell of bacon and eggs. She showered and changed into her favorite knee-length and flared flower print dress and faux leather church shoes. Her daddy was already seated at the table when she came down for breakfast.

"Good morning, baby girl. You finish your reading last night?"

"Yes, I did." She took her seat and brought the glass of orange juice to her mouth.

"What was it about?" he quizzed.

"World War I." She took a bite of her bacon and a spoonful of eggs.

"What did you learn?"

Serenity shrugged and her father put his fork down.

"When did it begin?"

"Nineteen-fourteen."

He smiled, impressed. "And when did it end?"

"Nineteen-eighteen."

"Beauty and brains." He chuckled, picking up his fork again. "You gonna be alright, baby girl."

Serenity entered the church just behind her father and they took seats in their usual pew two rows from the front. She took a quick look around and noticed Genesis and Miracle seated together towards the rear.

"Do you mind if I sit with my friends?" She asked when they waved her over.

"Go on." He smiled encouragingly. Serenity took up the seat on the other side of Genesis. Anyone looking at them would have thought the three were sisters. And that's how it was for them during the remainder of their fifth-grade year:

meeting up at school, church and the beauty salon, and then in the summer going to the park and the pool almost every day until their parents announced plans for their vacation.

"We're all going to Disney World?" They'd squealed together and Serenity felt her eyes widen as she looked to her father for confirmation.

"That's right," he assured her.

"All three of us? Me, Genesis, and Miracle?" She had to double check and make sure.

"Yes, we got a deal on a vacation through the church."

"Sweet!" she exclaimed.

Chapter Two: Dad the Coach

Serenity made it to the end of the workday, keeping the details of Miracle's coma in the back of her mind. A quick look at her reflection in the rearview mirror confirmed that her outward appearance was still calm and collected. She sat behind the wheel for a moment to think about her plans for the rest of the evening. She knew that a normal person would cancel all plans, go home, get drunk and have a good cry. But that sounded too close to being messy and out of control. If she allowed herself to spiral, there was no telling when, if ever, she would be able to pull out of it. She knew that it was better to remain calm and maintain her routine. She headed to the YMCA to work out and then coach the kids from the Boys and Girls Club.

She entered the workout room of the YMCA, adjusting her wireless headphones into place, and shutting out any and everything that had nothing to do with her pulse rate or the motion of the machines she used while in the gym.

As she stepped from the elliptical to work her arms on the dumbbells, she looked to the time on the wall indicating that she only had fifteen minutes until the Boys and Girls Club arrived. When she was done working out, she took the time to dry off her current layer of sweat before heading over to the gym to coach the kids. She hurried up the hall, remembering what it had been like trailing behind her father as he'd entered the same gym to coach the boys in the Amateur Athletic Union basketball team.

Between the summer she spent in Disney World with Genesis and Miracle, and the start of the next school year, the dynamics in their relationship had already begun to shift. The girls had all been given a long leash to run around and have fun on the resort as their parents rotated supervision of their activities. Serenity's father had made sure every day that she had a pocket full of money and cool gear to wear. She smiled, remembering that trip to Florida had been the first time she'd flown on a plane.

***

Serenity had spent two weeks shopping for new clothes and accessories to wear on vacation with her friends to Disney World. He'd allowed her to get several tank and short swimsuits as well as several pairs of sneakers, sandals, pool shoes, hats, and sunglasses. He'd also bought her first flip phone with a camera. She packed her favorite short sets and sundresses and felt as if she were a movie star as she stepped on a plane for the first time and took the window seat on her row, with Genesis in the middle and Miracle in the aisle seat. The girls held hands during both take off and touch down and between the two they'd taken trips to the bathroom, chewed through half a pack of bubble gum, eaten plane cookies with half a can of soda, watched a complimentary movie and drawn fake BFF tattoos on their ankles with permanent ink.

They piled into the back of the hotel shuttle pretending they weren't just within eyeshot of their parents and noisily pointed out cute boys on the street. It was even fun complaining about the weight of their luggage as they were put in charge of pulling their bags into the hotel and placing them in front of a bellboy in the lobby.

"This place is huge!" Genesis exclaimed as she turned in a circle looking upward in amazement. Serenity agreed, but tried to play it a little bit cooler as they stepped onto the glass elevator and rode with her dad to the twelfth floor. She couldn't remember ever being so high up. She gripped Genesis' hand for support as she began to feel anxious about being twelve stories up from the ground. When the doors opened behind them, letting them onto their floor, they bustled excitedly behind her dad to their expansive suite of rooms. They ran inside towards the large window facing the park.

"Where do we go first?" Miracle asked.

By the end of that first day, Serenity had blisters on both feet and was maybe five minutes from getting a sunburn. The rest of the vacation she made sure to stay lathered in sunblock and got used to the scent of chlorine mixed with ocean air. The day before they were to leave, Serenity woke with a stomachache and went to the bathroom to discover that she started her first period.

She wasn't sure exactly what to do. She knew that the bleeding was not going to stop for a few days at least and she didn't have the first supply. She asked both Genesis and Miracle who had camped out with her in the living room the night before, but they hadn't started yet. She took in a deep breath knowing that she was going to have to tell her dad. He was half asleep when he answered the door to his room.

"I started my period," she blurted out, certain that hemming and hawing would only make it worse.

His mouth dropped open and his eyes widened in surprise. "Okay..." He blinked several times and then, "I'll run to the store and be back shortly."

Her father was just as generous buying her supplies as he had been buying all the new things for her vacation. He handed the bag to her without saying much and she was able to clean herself up and finish up the last day of her vacation.

By the time school started, the words between herself and her father became more and more mature. Her father had begun coaching his third year of boys' basketball for the Amateur Athletics Union at the YMCA. He took her to his practices from time to time, and she enjoyed sitting behind the team and watching him coach during games. It was a new way for them to bond, getting away from the stress of school or his work. When the tournament rolled around, she was just as excited as he and the boys, wearing a fan jersey and painting half of her face in team colors.

She carried her father's clipboard and duffle bag, moving her feet double time behind her father's long strides as they made their way from the parking lot into the community center gym for the first in a series of tournament games to determine the final two teams that would enter the Championship. The muggy heat of late spring and early summer made it impossible to keep any hairstyle that did not involve cornrows or braids. That day, she had a cascade of micro braids pulled into a ponytail in the back of her head. Her father took his clipboard and duffle bag, handing her a ten-dollar bill for snacks and a drink during the game. She shoved the money into the pocket of her jean shorts before climbing on to the bleachers just behind them.

As soon as her dad dropped his duffle bag, the boys crowded around him a in a huddle momentarily shutting out the rest of the world, including Serenity. She didn't remember when it was that she realized his time with the boys of the team was in some way a replacement for the fact that he had not been blessed with a boy of his own. She herself even began to accept them as the brothers she didn't have. They lived in a good-sized town, but she knew enough of the boys on the team to understand that at least half of them didn't have fathers in their lives and at least one's father had recently passed away. She was proud of her dad for being one of the good men that stepped in to help keep them from becoming statistics. The space of time that encompassed their huddle was the only time she felt as if somehow she were not enough, however, without fail her father's eyes would find her on the bench immediately after. He would wink and pull his ear, and she would return the gesture for good luck.

Her dad's smile widened before turning back to the team's point guard. She could hear what he was saying, but let the sound of the words fall into the background as the hot dog vendor came to her row and sold her a foot-long with mustard. She knew that the coaching he gave to the young boys would be much the same as he gave her when they were just shooting in the backyard. He'd taught her what it meant to set a pick, how to block, how to avoid a double dribble and even how to shoot free throws, though she missed the hoop more than she made it. He was always patient while running after her rebounds and setting her up to shoot again.

"Any game you play can be considered a metaphor for life," he'd explained to her more than once. "Basketball consists of a team of players with very specific jobs. However, it is best if everyone playing can step in and do what needs to be done. So, in life you may find that you're working with a group and for whatever reason someone doesn't show up. Are you going to let the job fail or are you going to have what it takes to step in and do what needs to be done?"

"One monkey don't stop no show," she'd answered one time, making him laugh deep and rich at her response for the rest of the night.

"That's my baby girl," he'd said with genuine, unabashed pride.

Serenity made it halfway through her foot-long before another vendor showed up with cups of ice and soda. She bought one of each as she watched a player from the other team foul one of their players. This player was a particularly good shooter but still her dad took a moment to gently coach him on how to shoot. She imagined the words, *"Line the ball up with the post. Get your rhythm... Visualize this ball going into that net. You've done it before, you can do it again."*

At the end of the coaching he chucked the young man on the shoulder. Serenity felt a small twinge of jealousy, but let it pass. He'd chucked her on the shoulder plenty of times, even if it wasn't in the middle of a basketball tournament for all the world to see. Her eyes stayed on the player as he walked out to the free-throw line and set up his stance the way her father would have instructed. He lined up the ball with the post and bounced it several times to get his rhythm. Serenity bit her bottom lip as she, along with the remainder of the crowd, held her breath. The player bounced the ball one last time before pushing the ball off of his fingertips, letting it fly in a perfect arch into the net.

Serenity exhaled in relief only to pull in another breath as the ball was given back to the player. He set his stance again, and Serenity could hear herself quietly encouraging him, *"You've done it once... You can do it again."*

She held her breath once more as the ball sailed from his hands in another perfect arch into the net. The entire crowd behind the team cheered as the players all broke from the free throw set-up to continue the game. Her father gave the player an excited high five and Serenity took a sip of soda to wash down her hot dog wishing that she could high five or fist bump the player as well.

At half-time her father disappeared with the boys into the locker room. She took a break to visit the girls' room and get a box of candy from the concession stand. Along the way, she stopped by a display case with championship trophies from the previous two years, won under her father's coaching.

She looked at the pictures of the boys on the team for each year and noted that many of them had been on the team for two or three years. She gave a thought to what might have happened to them if they hadn't been on the team. There was no telling really. By then, she already knew that many black boys ended up in the system; juvenile detention, foster homes, or even jail, and many more than that never completed high school.

"It's as much about luck and opportunity as it is about self-determination," Her father had tried to explain to her. "There is a system that works hard against people that don't have a lot of money. But, we can determine for ourselves to do the work that it takes to be smart and become successful. Sometimes there are short cuts, but you have to determine for yourself if the risk is worth the reward."

Serenity moved on from the display case and entered the line for refreshments as the half-time clock ticked down to the final two minutes. When the teams returned, she watched the remainder of the game with great interest, watching as each team battled back and forth into overtime. When the clock wound down to the final seconds, their team had the ball and a small lead. The point guard took the ball to the net, but passed it just in time to miss a block and the other team member made the final shot. The crowd behind the team stood up in screams and cheers. Serenity's dad high-fived each player before turning to high-five her as well

"We're going to the Championships!" He cheered, and she jumped into his arms to give him a hug.

Chapter Three: The Plug's Daughter

Serenity had learned to appreciate the conversations she shared with her father. As she got older, he gave her more and more space to be on her own and hang out with friends. She understood that he was very interested in her life. While he kept his distance on some things, he also had to let her more and more into the world of his whole life.

She'd gone into the garage looking for a screwdriver and stumbled upon a supply of marijuana and other narcotic paraphernalia for distribution. She'd taken it out to get a better look and then tried to put everything back the way she'd found it. When she shut the drawer on the drugs, she wished that she could also shut it out of her mind. But, she must have not done it right. He'd patiently knocked on her door that night, which was unusual. If there were anything he needed to say and the door were closed, he'd just shout through it.

"Come in,' she'd answered, putting aside the magazine she'd been reading.

"Were you in the garage? And did you go through my things in the drawer?"

She'd nodded. "I thought I put it all back."

"You did and you're not in trouble. I just forgot to lock the drawer and wanted to talk to you if you had any questions or anything."

"No, I don't have any questions."

"Did you take any?"

"No, Daddy... It's drugs."

"Smart girl. I don't ever want you touching that stuff. You understand? It's a dead-end road."

"Then why do you have it?"

"I sell it to people."

"Why? I heard you say that stuff is poison. Why are you selling it?"

"The world is the way it is, and there's no amount of well-wishing or determination that's gonna change it."

"But, it's bad..." she'd trailed off, hoping that he would say something to refute what he was telling her and what she'd seen with her own eyes.

"Who gets to say what is bad or what is good?" he'd asked her instead.

"The law," she'd answered definitively.

"Whoever wins," he'd corrected her.

"What if you go to jail, Daddy?"

"Then I lose..."

"No, I lose," she'd corrected him.

"Your grandmother would take care of you, baby girl."

She exhaled. "Isn't it dangerous?"

"Yes, it's risky... But, the reward outweighs the risk. The money goes to the things we need and even donations to the church."

She could feel the lines of confusion creasing her brow as he continued.

"Everything... And I mean absolutely everything in this country is stacked against us. I'm a black man in the south... Nobody is going to hand me a white-collar job with a corner office and a salary sufficient enough to actually take care of myself and my family. I have to hustle. It can be dangerous, but so can living in poverty. Do you want to live in the projects over there?"

"No," she'd answered quickly, knowing that the HUD apartments were considered dangerous and he only wanted to take good care of her.

"If I could do it another way I would. But, this is all I got, Serenity. I'm not trying to live lavishly or abuse anyone. I just want to make sure you have what you need and we're okay."

She nodded as if she understood. But as an adult looking back, she knew that she hadn't had a clue, not at that time. Not when she'd gone off to college and not even when she'd had to drop out and get a job to pay her bills. It wasn't until the economy bottomed out, she lost her job and was actually facing the reality of moving into public housing that she truly understood how high the deck was stacked against her. When she'd driven to her father's old supplier in her Chevy Suburban and asked for a supply to help her get by, he'd been more than happy to help her set herself up in a suburban market. And it had been breathtakingly easy to do.

After spending three months job hunting, posting her résumé, and interviewing with no results, being handed a package and then finding parties to unload it all had been a piece of cake. She went from being flat broke and in the red to having over two grand in the bank in a matter of two weekends... and it only got better from there. Every time she made the run she heard her father's voice in her ear.

"Don't do anything in a routine and don't do anything in a rush."

As she left the YMCA with these words in her head, she reminded herself that she had a comfortable job with Vista Marketing and no longer needed to hustle. But, there was a comfort in knowing the extra money did go to good things. Equipment for the Boys and Girls Club basketball team for one, and donations to the school board's STEM initiatives for another. She wondered what Miracle would think of her if she knew. Would she judge her life choices?

She got into her car and sent a text to a client waiting on her weekend supply for a party at a club downtown. The traffic was always light after her time at the gym and the ride to the apartment building took less than twenty minutes. She put on her playlist, skipping directly to Stevie Wonder singing "Isn't She Lovely." Yesterday the song had drummed up thoughts and feelings for her father, and now her nostalgic and sad thoughts included Miracle.

Miracle was a lovely person inside and out. She was the type of person that could be the life of the party and center of attention or she could move behind the scenes and keep to herself. Serenity wished there was something in her that would break and allow her to cry. Feeling the turmoil didn't seem like enough. She should be weeping so hard that she could hardly drive, but she wasn't. Anyone looking at her would assume there was nothing out of the ordinary going on with her, even as she parked in front of her client's apartment and extracted a package wrapped in shiny paper and a ribbon. The apartments were nice enough. Serenity knew that if her client wanted to, she could upgrade to better. But, she was saving to put three kids through college and any splurging she did was at the spa and on her car. This run alone, Serenity would collect three thousand dollars in cash.

There was not a lot of small talk between the two of them as Serenity stepped into the spacious and tastefully decorated apartment.

"I just got back a few hours ago from taking the kids to their grandparents," her client shared with her. "Told them that I had a long weekend and they agreed to babysit."

Serenity smiled politely, not the chatty type herself, handing her the package and receiving a envelope full of cash. She wasn't eager to count it. She would most likely give it to Fortune to help with hospital costs anyway.

"Listen," she heard herself say without even thinking about it. "This is gonna be my last delivery."

"Oh?" Her client looked up in shock almost as it the news were unbelievable. "Why?"

"I umm... I just need to change some things around."

Her client gave a slow nod of understanding. "I get that. I wish I could change some things around. Well, thanks for letting me know. Can you recommend a new supplier?"

"I'll get you in touch with someone." Serenity waved goodbye as she headed for the door and back out of the apartment building. She made it halfway between the apartment building and her car before two police cars pulled in from opposite directions and stopped on either side of her.

She took a deep breath in and let it out, certain that even though her heartbeat raced erratically and a thin layer of perspiration appeared on her brow, she looked as cool as a cucumber. Four police officers lunged from the cars with weapons drawn on her. She put her hands in the air palms up praying that this would not be her last moment on this Earth.

"Serenity Brooks, get on the ground with your arms extended outwards!"

Serenity did as instructed forcing herself to breathe normally in order to avoid fainting or becoming light headed. An officer hurried to her side pulling one arm after the other behind her back and pinching a set of handcuffs on her wrists. The officer then helped her to her feet and began a pat down over her body that seemed more intimate than necessary until he extracted the envelope full of cash from her back pocket.

"Serenity Brooks, you are under arrest for possession and distribution of an illegal controlled substance. You have the right to remain silent. If you give up the right to remain silent, anything you say can and will be held against you in the court of law..."

Amazing

The joy you feel when you look back at where you were, what you've gone through, and how you made it! There is no way any obstacle can ever bring you down again because you know what's at the end of each trial and it feels amazing.

Dear Genesis,

I know it must be hard to have been left behind. I'm not sure why I stayed away so long but as I get ready to come back home, I can't even remember why it was I wanted to leave.

I can still remember all of the plans we all had when we were little girls. Spending time in your mom's beauty shop, watching her and your aunts do hair and make money made it seem like having anything in life was easy. Whenever I go to have my hair done now, I wish I had followed through on getting my beautician's license. I think back to those days in the salon, flipping through magazines, certain that we would be just as glamorous as the women in the pictures. And that we would each have our own long list of clients to work with, just like your mom and your aunts, working together, gossiping and giving good advice, making good money. Remember all of the nice things we were going to buy? If I ever get married, I still want to have matching BMWs like your parents. Riding with you in either one of them made me feel so special. You must have felt that way all of the time.

I know that we soon grew out of wanting to do hair and thought that we might be able to head out to Hollywood and be on kid's television, play-acting along to shows starring our favorite characters. Thinking that we could meet the Famous Jett Jackson. I know that they were farfetched, pie in the sky dreams but now they seem so pure and so simple. Even when we finally got over the Disney Channel and thought maybe we could come up with a cooking show of our own. I love thinking about how kind it was of your parents to let us make a mess in the kitchen, be an audience for our demonstrations and then bravely taste test what we came up with.

It would be nice if we could go back, even for a little while, wouldn't it? A time when everything was so simple and everyone that we loved was still with us. I can remember being in such a rush to grow up and move away. Now, I wish that I could come home and just stay. We were really fortunate weren't we, Genesis?

Please write back and let me know that you're okay.

Love,

Strength

PATIENCE

- *(noun) - the capacity to accept or tolerate delay, trouble, or suffering without getting angry or upset.*

Chapter One: The Skin I'm In

Patience Thomas placed her suitcase in the trunk of her car and slammed it shut a little harder than necessary before getting behind the wheel and pulling out of the driveway. It was just after sunrise and the rosy orange tint of the sun flooded her car. She adjusted the visor on both sides of the windshield to protect her eyes from any potential glaring and turned the radio to her favorite early morning show. But, even the songs, jokes and laughter of the on-air personalities were not enough to pull her out of the anger and frustration of the day that was ahead of her. In fact, her day had started in the middle of the night, when a collect call from the county jail announced that one of her lifelong friends, Serenity Brooks, was on the line.

"You're kidding me, right?" Patience wished that she could be the carefree and easy breezy type to handle any crisis without an attitude, but she wasn't. She was certain that somewhere in some dictionary under the term "Angry Black Woman," there was a picture of her that got updated every three months to match her social media profile. It wasn't that Patience was angry, not really. She just couldn't suffer fools for long, and what Serenity was calling her from jail about was just as foolish as anything she'd ever heard.

"I need someone to come and bail me out."

"Someone? Like who?"

"Patience, can you please come and bail me out of jail?"

"Honey, you really have no idea how the system works, do you?"

"No..." Serenity had trailed off and the anxiety in her voice was apparent.

Good, Patience thought to herself. *Maybe she'll think twice before breaking the law.*

"Sweetie, you are in there for the night at least. You have to face the judge and bail has to be set before I can come get you."

"But, you will come?"

"Yes, of course. I'll have a lawyer meet you before you see the judge. Just do as she says."

Serenity had thanked her and agreed to do as she was told before hanging up. Even though she didn't agree with what Serenity had done, she did feel bad for her that she would have to spend the night in jail. She took her time to say a prayer for her friend before going back to sleep.

As the traffic in front of her began to slow down, Patience looked to the clock on her dashboard. She was going to be late for the arraignment if she didn't miss it altogether. She'd gotten on the phone first thing that morning to call in favors to get a lawyer to represent Serenity. So at least she would be in good hands. But she still had to get to the bank and withdraw at least a thousand dollars for Serenity's bail. Patience shook her head, knowing that if Miracle were able to handle this situation, she would have been able to do it with more loving-kindness and understanding. That's what made having her as a friend so great. She could put anyone at ease about anything. That is the way it had been when they were just kids and Patience was going through a particularly rough experience with eczema.

Patience began to smile even as tears pricked her eyes as she thought about the early days of her friendship with Miracle. Just as she began to relax and accept the snail's pace of the stop and go traffic, the driver behind her decided not to pay attention and rammed right into the back of her car. She cursed out loud and picked up her cell phone to take pictures of any damages and get ready to call the police.

When she got out of the car and looked at the dent on her bumper, she tried to channel Miracle's calm demeanor, but failed. As she took the other driver's information and called the police for an accident report, it was her mother's voice that came to soothe her nerves and calm her frustration.

***

"You will be just fine..." Patience's mother reassured her as she rubbed ointment into a patch of eczema on the back of her hand. Patience tried not to panic at the thought of going to the first day of junior high school with a fresh flare-up.

"It wouldn't be so bad if I were going to Wesley Middle School with my friends," Patience murmured, trying not to be too angry about the choice her mom had made to send her to school in another neighborhood.

"I know it seems unfair, but going to Jackson Academy, you'll have more exposure and choices, resources and opportunities."

"I also have to wake up an hour earlier to catch the school bus, Mom."

"You will get used to it. Come on, Dad made breakfast."

Patience only nibbled on her food and drank a little bit of OJ until it was time to walk to the corner and catch the bus. The jeans and long sleeves that she wore to cover up most of her eczema were a little uncomfortable as it was still hot and muggy outside, but she preferred to suffer the heat over suffering strange stares and worried looks from strangers.

She didn't have to stand on the corner too long before the bus turned onto her street and stopped to pick her up. She climbed onto the bus and took the first empty seat that she came by and looked out of the window without taking the time to see who else was on the bus. She covered the spot on her hand with her other hand and watched as the local landmarks passed by. She looked at the bus door at every stop to see if she recognized anyone and after three stops, she did. It was Miracle.

They hadn't been super close friends before, but as she entered the bus she smiled at Patience and Patience smiled back in relief as she took the seat next to her. Patience relaxed a little, still keeping her hand covered and they chatted the rest of the ride over. When they got to the school, they found out they were in the same homeroom class. Once they got to homeroom, they noticed Serenity already seated inside. After a few classes together, Patience realized that it would be impossible to keep her hand covered all the time and by the time they made it to the science lab, Miracle and Serenity had gotten a good look at her rash and not seemed bothered or even curious. Patience was able to relax and stop thinking so much about what others thought of her and took a good look around at what the school that her mother was so impressed with had to offer.

The school was large with state-of-the-art computers, a science lab, a library, art room, music room, and fully renovated gym. Those first few weeks getting around were difficult. Her eczema was not getting any better.

"Aren't you hot in those clothes?" Serenity had been the one to point out the obvious.

"Yes, but, I don't want people staring at my breakouts."

"They aren't that bad," Serenity had commented.

"Leave her alone," Miracle had intervened. "It can't be easy having people stare."

'Not at all,' Patience had agreed. "Some of them don't think that I notice but I do and it does make me uncomfortable. When the flare up ends then I'll be able to wear shorts and short sleeve shirts."

Patience had gone home that day feeling a little worse than usual. She thought about everything she had done to try and get rid of her flare-ups. She took medicine, rubbed in ointment, and even bathed in oatmeal to try and help her skin heal.

"I don't know even one other person with eczema," she complained to her grandmother when she went for a visit to help her with her garden. "Why do I have to be the one with this condition?"

"Everything we go through in this life is meant to make us stronger," her grandmother had answered.

"I don't want to be stronger," she'd countered. "I want to be comfortable and I want to fit in."

"Maybe that's something you will have to think about... The need to fit in."

"You don't understand. It's not that I want to be popular. I'd rather just be ordinary and blend in."

"You want to be invisible?"

"I'd prefer that to what's going on now."

"Well, that's not good either."

"You just don't understand," Patience said again.

"Well, of course I do. I was young once too, you know. I didn't always have this grey hair up here."

"But, you never had to deal with a skin rash."

"You got me there... I only had to deal with segregation, Jim Crow, pre-civil rights racism, sexism and lack of resources." She smiled sweetly at Patience, who was not lost on what her grandmother was trying to say.

"I know."

"Do you?"

"I do."

"Good, because as bad as what you're going through may seem, it could always be worse, and I can guarantee that it actually is or has been worse for somebody else."

Chapter Two: Room 711

Patience made her way through security of the courthouse and to the courtroom with just a few minutes to spare. It was early, but she was still surprised to see that only a fraction of the seating made available for the public was filled. She looked to the front of the courtroom to see that the judge had yet to arrive. She spotted Deborah Washington, a private defense attorney she'd met through professional networking events. She smiled encouragingly at Patience and waved her to take a seat next to her.

She gave Patience a brief but strong hug and then leaned back. Patience could feel the worry etched in her face as Deborah continued to smile encouragingly.

"Everything is going to be fine," she reassured her. "This is a first offense and a non-violent crime. I've advised her to plead not guilty. The judge will set bail and ask for a trial to be scheduled. I doubt that it will be more than a thousand dollars."

"I have it," Patience let her know.

"Good. After the arraignment, you can pay the bail in the business office and then go to the jail house to collect Serenity."

"Okay."

"I will work with the prosecution's office to get the charges reduced to misdemeanor possession. And then we will negotiate probation and some volunteer hours. That is the best-case scenario."

"That's a lot better than what she was facing. Thanks, Debbie."

"You're very welcome."

"All rise."

Patience stood up alert as the judge entered the courtroom and took his seat behind the bench. When they were seated again, the public defender's cases, which took less than an hour were heard first. Then Serenity's name was announced, and Patience felt her anxiety level begin to rise. Deborah took her place at the defense table as Serenity was escorted in an orange jumpsuit and handcuffs to the seat next to her. Patience didn't realize how shallow her breathing had become as she looked at Serenity's hair, usually styled to perfection, now pulled back in a plain ponytail, and her face, usually piled with layers of makeup, clean and washed out against the bright orange of her jumpsuit. If Patience hadn't known it was her, she would have never recognized her, and she would have taken her for any other common criminal.

The hearing took less than five minutes. The prosecution read the charges. The judge asked a few questions. Serenity finally replied, "Not guilty."

When it was all over, Serenity was escorted out of the court and Deborah came back to Patience, signaling that they could leave.

When Serenity exited the jail house, her wig was back in place and she'd taken the time to apply a light coat of makeup.

"How was your stay?" Patience asked sarcastically as Serenity slid into the passenger seat.

"Well, a lot like sleep away camp," she answered with a slight shrug.

Patience shook her head.

"I called into work. The police searched my office. So, now I'm out of a job."

"I'm sorry, Serenity," Patience said, knowing now was not the time to give her a lecture.

"My friend is dying. I spend a night in jail. I lose my job... Trouble always comes in threes."

"You're sure right about that," Patience agreed as she thought about her last days of sixth grade. Her dad had come to pick her up with news of her grandfather passing away.

***

"Please send Patience to the front office for early dismissal."

The announcement came over the P.A. system as she sat in science class. She was stunned as her parents never came to pick her up early. Miracle and Serenity gave her concerned looks as she collected her belongings. She gave a slight shrug, not certain what was going on.

But in the back of her mind she knew that her mother's health had suddenly become a concern as she'd lately been too weak to stay an entire day at work and spent most weekends in bed or on the sofa. She headed to her locker feeling a little shaky as she collected the rest of her things and hurried to the front office. She imagined every possible thing that could be wrong until she and her father were in his car and he finally spoke to her.

"Your grandfather suffered a heart attack this morning."

"Oh." She was stunned. "Is he okay?"

"He was rushed to the hospital. Unfortunately, he passed away."

A wave of sadness hit her. "How's mom?" she asked, knowing that he understood her question had two meanings.

"She's sad of course. But, she's alright."

Patience nodded her understanding.

The car seemed unusually quiet as he drove back across town to her grandmother's house. Whenever they made a stop, he would turn to her and offer words of comfort that she was certain were as much for his benefit as her own.

"He lived a long and full life," he stated at one stop. And then, "Now he's at peace. Resting."

Her grandfather had always seemed well-rested and peaceful as he got older. He looked so mean and you could tell he didn't play games back in his day; but he was so pure hearted and hardworking, she thought as the car continued along. At the stop just before her grandma's house, he said, "It was just his time."

These words of comfort would come back to Patience from time to time as her mother's health continued to decline. She'd been able to walk on her own to her grandfather's service and made it through the burial and repast. However, the exertion of the day had taken a toll that she'd never been able to bounce back from. It seemed little more than a blink of the eye before her mother became too sick to work at all and then was rushed by ambulance to the hospital.

She spent her final days in the hospital with bouts of welcome energy followed by stretches of listlessness. Prior to her health taking a turn for the worse, her dad had purchased tickets for them to see Gerald Levert live in concert.

"I hate that we have to miss it," she'd apologized.

"Says who?" he'd asked, and produced a radio tuned to the live broadcast.

Her smile had been as bright as the sun as he took a seat next to her while Patience sat at the foot of the bed to listen. She watched her father mouth some of the words, gently touching her mother's arm or kissing her forehead at intervals. Her mother's happy smile beamed towards her and her father in turn throughout the concert. Patience could feel her thoughts and emotions turn inwardly. Understanding that her mother was dying, she tried to remember the words of comfort her father had offered at her grandfather's passing. Had her mother lived a full life? How could it possibly be her time so soon after her grandfather passed away? But she could see that her mother was tired from her battle. She needed relief from the pain: mental, emotional, and physical. She was ready to welcome her rest.

When the songs came to an end, Patience and her father left her mother sleeping peacefully. They returned the next day, what would have been her last day of sixth grade if she'd gone. It seemed to Patience that everyone was there to say their goodbyes. Her mother took the time to speak to them all. She waited her turn and when her mother's eyes fell on her she walked to her side and took her hand. She listened intently as the last words her mother would speak to her fell softly from her lips.

"You will always be my baby," she told her at the end. She used the little strength she had to pull Patience into her arms, and though Patience was sure she used every ounce of strength she had to try and squeeze her tight and hold her close, the embrace was soft and tender.

She listened intently as her mother shared words with the rest of the family, taking it all in as she asked an older cousin that Patience looked up to to look out for her. When she'd gone around the room, her grandmother entered, and Patience witnessed a peaceful relief wash over her mother's face. She realized she'd been holding on and waiting for her to arrive.

When they finished speaking, her grandmother stood, giving her hand back to her father. Her mother's eyes traveled to her father and then they looked up to the ceiling. They fluttered as the machines behind her bed began to ring an alarm. One of the relatives moved to the door, calling for the nurse. But her father's raised hand waved them back. The distraction took Patience's eyes from her mother for only a moment, and when she looked back, her mother's eyes were closed.

The flatline whine of the machine triggered a growing murmur of grief-stricken relatives. But Patience couldn't find the will to grieve or cry. Looking at her mother, she knew that she was gone and all she could do was turn away and look anywhere else. Her eyes fell on the door and the room number etched in gold, room 711.

Chapter Three: Moving On

Patience followed Serenity into her apartment and stopped short when the ransacked mess came into view. She had not been prepared to come face to face with the mess left behind after the police department searched the place for more evidence against Serenity.

"If my office looked anything like this once they were done, no wonder I got fired," Serenity took a half-hearted crack at making a joke. But it was very apparent to Patience that she was shaken to see the chaos of her life so blatantly on display.

"Do you think they found anything?" she asked with cautious concern.

"No, I never keep the stash in my apartment."

"Where—never mind." Patience thought better than to ask the question.

"Usually in my locker at the Y. But, I'd dropped off my last bit just before the arrest."

"You think she turned on you?"

"Yeah, most likely. It was a routine that I should have broken long ago. In holding, they came to ask me a lot of questions and revealed how much they knew."

"I see."

"I'm not proud of it."

"I know."

Serenity let out a heavy sigh.

"What do you want to do? About the mess, I mean," Patience asked her.

"Nothing right now. It'll still be here for me when I get back. They have my car. Is it okay if I ride with you to meet up with the others?"

"Of course."

"Just give me time to take a real shower and throw some clothes in a bag."

Patience couldn't force herself to sit still in the messy apartment as she listened to the knocks and bumps of Serenity taking a shower and then packing up. She busied herself with pulling the sofa pillows off the floor and putting them back in place. She then moved on to stacking mail and stray papers nice and neatly onto the dining room table and washing the few dishes that were left in the sink. By the time Serenity was ready to go, the entryway of the apartment looked as if nothing was wrong at all. But, even though she hadn't taken a step into the hallway to look at the bedrooms or the bathrooms, she knew there was still a mess. That's the way life is. Just beneath the surface, just behind the curtain, just beyond view there was another mess waiting.

As they got back into the car, it wasn't lost on her how similar the quiet calm of putting part of Serenity's home back together was to the quiet calm of dismantling the material possessions her mother left behind.

***

Patience felt as if nothing about the first few months without her mother felt right. The air was too still. The house was too big. Her room was too cold. And her father... Well, she could never find the words to describe what her father had become too much of in those months. It would take Patience more than a decade of wading through her own pain and the confusion of her own grief before she'd be able to put the right words to how her father had changed and which parts of himself he'd buried the day they'd laid her mother to rest.

Early in the months that followed, Patience's godmother, Tracey, stepped in to fill in as much of her mother's shoes as she could. She'd begun by taking the time to help Patience and her father look through, throw out, give away, and hold onto her mother's belongings. Many of the fine clothes, with brand names and even the tags in some cases, ended up donated to Goodwill or given to her aunts along with much of her costume jewelry. Her diamonds were given to Patience's grandma and then to Patience. Many of the odds and ends and some personal items that weren't thrown away or donated ended up with various family friends and relatives. There wasn't much from her mother's things that she wanted to keep. It was mostly just stuff. However, when she came across a pack of invitations with Tweety Bird printed on them, she felt her heart flutter and for the first time a nostalgic smile touched her lips, pushing away just for a moment, the dark shadows of sorrow surrounding her heart.

It had been a crystal-clear spring day, somewhere between the icy chill of late winter and the unrelenting heat of early summer, when they'd gone for a late lunch in town. Maybe there had been some hint that her mother wasn't feeling well, the slowed cadence of her speech or the barely touched chicken salad she'd ordered. But she'd been just as excited as Patience to come across the last pack of Tweety Bird invitations in the store and set about collecting matching cups and napkins, paper plates and plastic cutlery to go with it for a weekend slumber party. That's when she realized how many things like that she would miss, the little details that her mother paid attention to and added up to so much more than expected.

She'd lie in bed at night, quietly listing little details her mother took care of that she'd taken for granted. It became nearly impossible for her to sleep at all in her own bed or anywhere else in the house that had ghostly memories of her mother in every corner. It was so difficult that she began spending nights at her grandmother's house for two or three day stretches at a time. Upon returning for clean clothes and belongings, she'd begun to notice things missing. Her mother's easy chair and then the television in the guest room were the most obvious empty spaces. Then she'd returned one Sunday after church to find that her mother's car was no longer in the driveway.

"Why?" she'd asked after her father admitted to selling it. She'd been prepared for him to say that he sold it because he no longer needed it. She wasn't sure what she would have responded, but she knew that it wouldn't have been anything charitable. But, that's not the answer he gave. The loss of the car had felt abruptly cold and shocking. But his response was even more chilling.

"With your mom gone, things are getting tight. I just couldn't afford to keep it."

"Oh..." had been her whispered response as her grief and loneliness took on the added stress of her father's financial insecurity. She didn't yet have the words to express the feeling which foreshadowed the day neither she nor her father had a house to come back to.

Dividing up their own material possessions, much the same way they had done with her mother's, had been a bitter pill filled with lessons of tragedy and poverty. Her godmother had stepped in once again to help her with the monumental task of getting rid of over half of her things.

"How much am I supposed to lose?" she'd asked her, and her godmother knew right away she wasn't talking about the things. Her face became a mixture of sadness and sympathy.

"Every life has its seasons. Sometimes the best things happen to us for no good reason, and it can be just the same when the worst things happen to us."

The words had not been comforting in the moment, and much less so when she set eyes on the double wide trailer her father had rented in a completely different neighborhood and zip code. As he drove her from the familiar comfort of her grandmother's house to the seemingly joyless setting of the trailer, she couldn't help but wonder if somehow she'd been forced to leave part of herself behind as well. She wondered how long she could walk in the darkness of so much uncertainty. She couldn't deal with not knowing the answer. She was done with the quiet chaos and confusion. She didn't want to be brave or understanding. She was tired of being sad and feeling as if she were lost and always alone.

She couldn't do it anymore. So she didn't. She stayed at her grandmother's house as often as she could while her dad started working. Leaving all the pain and fear and uncertainty in the strangeness of that trailer that could never be her home. She left it all behind. Allowing herself to deny that any of it existed. So long as she didn't have to look at it, she could just ignore it.

Evaluate

Once we realize what our challenges are, we then need to recognize our strengths. Once we accomplish that, we need to separate the two, work on them and allow our strengths to WIN!

Dear Genesis,

After all these years, I can still remember how fearless you were when we were kids. It must be thanks to how wonderfully loving and protective your parents were. You could stand up to any challenge and weren't afraid to sing and dance whenever the mood hit you.

Even swinging on the playground, you'd pump your legs as hard as possible. You'd go high enough that you nearly fell out of the swing more than once. And do you remember when we came up with the contest of leaping from the swing while it was still in motion and high up in the air? We would measure to see who could land the furthest away from the swing set. If anyone ever got further than you, you would try again until you were back in the lead.

The only time I ever remember you being scared was the day we came upon a stray dog on our way home. Of course, all the kids were scared, but you were so frightened you couldn't even move at first and the other kids had to pull you along to get out of the dog's path. It seemed strange to me, since you had a dog of your own, Blue. But you told me a few years later that your Aunt Patrice was also afraid of dogs. You said she was so afraid that when a small dog ran from the house towards her at a family gathering, it frightened her so much that she had a stroke. You and your entire family were devastated when the stroke led to an aneurysm that required brain surgery.

That was around the time you found out you were adopted. The way you described it to me, your father took you for a ride in his black Chevrolet with Blue in the back seat and explained it to you. It's normal that your first concern was that you might have to go away. It must have taken you some time to process the news and then ask. But your father said, "Hell no! You are ours and you're not going anywhere." His words made you feel secure and he let you know that you didn't have to tell anyone about being adopted if you didn't want to. I know that you didn't for a long time.

Write back, Genesis, and let me know how you're doing?

Love Always,
Strength

FORTUNE

- *(noun)* - *chance or luck as an external, arbitrary force affecting human affairs.*

Chapter One: Poker Face

"No, it's not gonna be easy. As a matter of fact, I'm gonna go ahead and tell you that it's gonna be extremely difficult. And you..." Fortune paused for dramatic effect as she pointed to the sea of people in the audience. "You will have to do... the... work." She punctuated the last three words with a pause as well, making sure to face each area of the audience as she did. She took a step back from the podium, still amazed that the pricey designer shoes she wore felt so comfortable. She walked towards the edge of the stage, giving the audience of nearly eight hundred people the feeling that she wanted to be close to them, and bring them into her confidence.

"We all read our Bible, right?" she nodded affirmatively as she asked the question. "So, we all know that the same God that lives in me... He lives in you too. The same God that took all of my trials and hard circumstances and turned them into my success lives in you. I didn't achieve any of the success you see in me on my own, and you are not on your own either. You have the same potential to transform your life and become whatever it is that you want."

Fortune paced to one side of the stage. "I want everyone in here to close your eyes. With your eyes closed, I want you to think about and visualize what it is that you really want for your life." Fortune began walking towards the other side of the stage, letting her eyes roam over the audience. However, she stopped short as she came to the center of the stage and noticed Strength sitting in the front row with her eyes wide open. She was glad that everyone else had their eyes closed as she took a moment to recover from the renewed wave of grief she'd been holding back since stepping on stage.

She'd had to put the fresh pain of Miracle's coma in the back of her mind and be there for her audience. Her heart fluttered uneasily as she struggled to regain her composure.

She bit down on her bottom lip, not certain how much longer the audience would sit quietly with their eyes closed. She took in a breath, closing her own eyes and counting backwards from ten as she let the onslaught of grief and long buried memories rush in.

***

There were not many young girls that lived in the trailer park, so Fortune took notice of Patience when she moved in. Patience was a girl that always seemed to be in a hurry to be anywhere but there when she was home. She understood the feeling, but knew they both had a long time to wait before they could leave. It took a while for Fortune to get Patience to open up about her life before moving to the trailer park.

"There just seems to be a before and after. Before the trailer my life was good. I had everything and everyone that I needed."

Fortune could see the pain in her eyes as she avoided talking about her mother passing away. Patience figured that maybe it was easier for Fortune to see things in terms of before moving as opposed to before she lost her mother. Maybe it was easier to feel frustrated by what must have been a massive downgrade. Fortune took her on a tour of the neighborhood, introducing her to the neighbors so she would feel a little bit better about the people if not the surroundings.

"There's just a certain feeling I would get walking to my house to or sitting in the back seat as my parents pulled out of the driveway. Belonging to that neighborhood and having that zip code made me feel untouchable."

"No one actually wants to live in a trailer park, Patience," she'd said quietly one day.

"I know. The people are nice. I just don't feel like I belong here. What did I ever do to deserve this?"

"What did you ever do to deserve the life you had before?"

"Nothing, I just..." Patience fell quiet looking more and more thoughtful.

"You've lost a lot. I know. I can't tell you how many times I've looked at other neighborhoods and wondered why I couldn't live in one of those brand new mini-mansions. It must be something to have a nice big house to invite friends to after school or for sleepovers. But this place isn't so bad, and we at least have a hope."

What hope is there? Other than my grandma's house, I have nowhere else to go."

"If we want out, we gotta have a plan."

"You mean like hustling?"

"No, I don't mean like hustling." Fortune had been annoyed by the question. "We have to finish school and go to college."

"And then what?"

Fortune had shrugged. "Anything we want. I'm gonna write a book about my life here."

"Good luck with that," Patience had responded with less interest than Fortune cared for. She went on into details, knowing that Patience was probably ignoring every word that she spoke, but she knew that the more often she said the words out loud, the easier it was to keep the vision alive and the more likely her plan would work.

In truth, her plan was all that she had to hold on to. Like Patience, it was just herself and her dad living in the trailer. Once upon a time he talked about plans to leave, but it seemed as if one thing after another stole away his hope for himself. But, that didn't stop him from pushing for Fortune to work hard and reach for the stars. She knew that most people didn't want to hear what must have seemed like her pipe-dream, so she mainly kept it to herself. And with nothing else to focus on, she was mainly reserved and stayed to herself. It was easy for people to think of her as shy and she let them do that, rather than to explain her vision... her plan for how to get out of the trailer park.

Even if she didn't realize it, her focus on her plan and getting out of that trailer park was stressful. Every day seemed like a mental marathon that included everything she had to do in a day from brushing her teeth to studying for tests. The amount of pressure that she put on herself, striving for what others termed black excellence, had led to her skin breaking out and her hair, which had once been long, breaking off. She worried too much about what people might think of her, especially since she also wore boy-style clothes. She couldn't imagine her dad taking her clothes shopping or giving him a list of girl clothes to get for her, so she just kept it simple unless her grandma brought her stuff.

Living in the trailer was not ideal, but it was better than living on the streets, since they still had a little space and a yard where she could tend to a small container garden when the weather was not too hot or too cold. It was a good place to think and let the stress of her everyday melt away. Working on her own, she didn't have to say, do, or be anything other than a girl in her garden. She didn't even feel the need to think of her plans for the future that was still so far away from her. The soil and seeds were easy. At school, there were right clothes, right shoes, the right hair, the right grades, the right scores, the right friends. In the garden there was only water, soil, seeds, and sun. She was young, but still she understood that nature was simple, but life in junior high was hard. She'd witnessed a boy busted with a gun being arrested and taken away from school in handcuffs. She'd seen more than one girl withdraw from school when their pregnancy began to show. She'd been too close to more than a few schoolyard or hallway fights. But there was one day that Fortune knew was a turning point for the rest of her life.

It is unclear how the idea came up or whose idea it was, but late spring in eighth grade, she and Patience decided to cut class after lunch period and hang around the gym to watch boys play ball. Fortune didn't find any of the boys

JAIRA B. WILLIAMS

particularly interesting but, the thrill of being in the gym when she was supposed to be in class caused a welcomed shift in her stress level. She and Patience sat behind a few players on the girls' team as they watched the boys' game. At some point someone passed her a small bag with what looked like medicine. When she realized that what she had in her hand was drugs, everything around her slowed down. She thought about the resource officers roaming the hall—what if she got caught arrested and kicked out of school?

Someone nudged her shoulder and she looked up to the girl beside her. "Pass it over," she hissed. Fortune had never felt so relieved to empty her hands. She turned her attention to Patience, who'd witnessed the exchange.

"I think maybe we should get back to class," Patience suggested.

"I thought those were your friends." Fortune said as they left the gym.

"No not really, just girls that I know."

"But, you want to be friends with them?"

"No, not anymore. It's better to be alone than in bad company. If my mom is watching over me, I wouldn't want to disappoint her."

From then on, Fortune always went to class. For the remainder of junior high school, she tried to hide behind a hard shell in public and only really hung out with Patience. She felt that keeping to herself would keep her from having to fit in with other girls at school as well as keep her away from negative distractions such as drugs and boys. Every adult she ever talked to urged her to understand that getting a good education and going to college were the keys to success. It wasn't always easy, however, she always kept her head up and was never concerned about being singled out.

Then everything changed when she entered high school and met Miracle. Patience had talked about her friends from her old school before. They were still in touch but hadn't had an opportunity to hang out or reconnect since she'd moved across town. But she had brightened up beyond belief when she learned that they would be going to high school with Miracle. As soon as Fortune met her, she understood why.

"You have the perfect bone structure for short cuts," she'd complimented her out of the blue as they hung out after school flipping through magazines.

"Really?" Fortune asked doubtfully. She'd spent so much time feeling awkward about her short hair which continued to break off from stress.

"Yep." Miracle had shoved a magazine with a model sporting a short haircut. "That would be hot on you."

Miracle was a welcome breath of fresh air that distracted Fortune from her obsessive thoughts about finishing school and getting out of the trailer—at least for a little while. Miracle was the type of friend that made Fortune want to slow down and enjoy the journey. There didn't seem to be a point in rushing to adulthood as long as they were laughing and joking together.

"Do you think your dad would let you come to the mall with us? Patience and I want to get new dresses for Serenity's house party."

"I guess he might," Fortune had responded, not certain if he would or wouldn't but he seemed pleased when she did ask.

"Of course. How much do you think you'll need?" Fortune wasn't sure, so he gave her a hundred dollars.

"I am not gonna spend a hundred dollars on a dress, Dad."

"Well then get a few other things and buy food or something. Enjoy yourself."

"Thanks!" she couldn't remember him ever handing her so much money before.

She caught the bus to the mall with Patience and Miracle and felt herself relax as she sat between them chatting back and forth about music, clothes, hair, and boys.

"Who do you think is cute?" Miracle asked her.

"I don't know. I don't think about boys like that," Fortune admitted.

"Really?" Miracle seemed surprised. "I am completely boy crazy." Fortune smiled to see that she wasn't afraid to admit that at all. "I bet if you gave any one of them the time of day they would fall all over themselves for you."

"No..."

"Girl, yes!"

Fortune looked at the long pants and t-shirt she wore, not feeling as confident in herself as Miracle seemed. As they strolled from store to store, Miracle helped her navigate to the clearance racks "In order to get the biggest bang for your buck," she'd explained. "The problem with clothes, especially girl clothes, is that they really are not made to last. So why pay a fortune for something that you might wear only five or six times before it begins to fall apart?"

"Right," Fortune agreed, even though she'd never thought about it that way.

Miracle chose three outfits and a dress for Fortune to try on. "You have such a cute figure. You should show it off."

"Nah, it's not me," Fortune had explained even as she ran a hand over the soft fabric and looked herself over in the mirror. She agreed that the clothes she'd picked out for her were flattering.

"Well, you have to wear that dress to Serenity's party."

"You don't think that it makes me look goofy?"

"Goofy? Are you joking? No way! Girl, you look good!"

Chapter Two: Independence

Fortune pressed a cool smile to her lips as she pushed beyond the flood of memories and emotions to complete her motivational speech. After the initial surprise of seeing Strength seated in the audience, she settled back into her cool-as-a-cucumber public persona, and completed her presentation as she had dozens of times before with ease. As she came to the end of her speech, she thanked the audience and waved goodbye before she headed off stage. She let her eyes deliberately travel back to Strength's seat only to find that she was no longer there. It was surprising to see that she hadn't noticed her exit and wondered if she'd only imagined her in the first place.

She shook off her uncertainty as her publicist, Kim, met her backstage and quickly ushered her back to the dressing room to change for a media networking party in another room. Kim rattled off a to-do-list that Fortune did not have the energy to pay attention to, let alone keep up with. She nodded her agreement to the publicist's ideas as she handed herself over to the makeup and wardrobe team. It was odd how she'd gotten used to not being certain who it was that unzipped her dress, or slipped off her shoes, or wrapped her up in a terry cloth robe before she took a seat in front of a large mirror.

She braced herself as her wig was removed and the makeup artist stepped in to patch up the havoc of smudges and perspiration. She looked over the make-up artist's palate of primer, foundation and colors. It was indeed a long way from the box-store brand of makeup that lined the desk of her room in her trailer.

***

"What time are you gonna be home tonight?" Fortune's dad asked as she checked her hair and makeup in the hall mirror. She'd taken a chance on a pixie hair cut that made her eyes and cheek bones look dangerously sexy.

"Looking like Angela Bassett," Miracle declared. "Chris gonna notice you, girl!"

Chris was a boy in their class that she mentioned one time after watching him play ball. She hadn't said much to him all year and doubted that he even knew her name. But once she said something Miracle pounced on the chance to invite him to Serenity's party.

"Serenity's dad isn't gonna let the party last beyond nine o'clock. So, I'll catch the nine-thirty back across town and be here before ten."

"Okay." Her dad looked proud and worried at the same time. "And if you think that you will be even a minute late, what do you do?"

"I will call and let you know."

"Yes. Call the house. Let me hear your voice."

"You got it, Dad."

She could tell that her father would prefer if she stayed home so that he knew she was safe. But he'd given her more and more freedom and independence after her fifteenth birthday and even more when she'd gotten her driver's license. He let her borrow his car from time to time, but she preferred to take the bus across town and relax as she watched buildings, houses and landscapes pass by. It gave her time to think about what she wanted to do and where she wanted to live when she finally got out of high school and graduated from college. Her dad also really liked Patience and Miracle. He knew that they would both look out for her at the party.

"Call," he reiterated as Patience knocked on the door. "No texting and no e-mail."

"I promise to call," she reassured him as she gave him a hug and he hugged her back.

"You girls stay together," he instructed as he let her go.

"Wow, girl! Where you get those earrings?" Patience asked as they strolled in the late afternoon sun towards the bus stop.

"They were on sale at the Chinese store," Fortune told her.

"I need to get me a pair like that."

Fortune let her comment go unanswered as they reached the bus stop to join two other people waiting as well. When the six-thirty from across town arrived, they stepped to the side as a sea of commuters coming home from work disembarked. She and Patience headed straight to the back and took up the last seat.

"It's always so overwhelming to see all of those buildings and people," Patience commented as they both looked out of the window at people who seemed to have better lives and opportunities than they had themselves.

"One day that will be us," Fortune assured her. "We'll be whoever we want. Live wherever we want. Do whatever we want."

"What you think you'll do when you finish college?" Patience asked.

"I'm still not sure," Fortune admitted, feeling a small sense of anxiety even though she still had two years of high school and four years of college left before she had to figure out what she wanted to do. "I would like a job where I could help people. How about you?"

"Girl, you know I have a hard time thinking past what I want to do today, let alone what I want to do a decade from now. I think I'll just be happy to graduate and work at the mall."

Fortune nodded. "That's a thought. You know, we could get part-time jobs there this summer. And if you keep working there part-time, by the time you graduate you could get a full-time position and maybe be put on a management track."

"Wow, you really do think ten steps ahead don't you?" Patience commented.

Fortune chuckled, a little embarrassed.

"For the rest of the night, I don't want you to think about the future. Just think about tonight. Flirt with Chris and dance until you sweat out that 'do.'"

"I'll try my best," Fortune promised. But it was hard for her not to constantly think about the things she wanted that other people seemed to have.

When they got off the bus, they began the leisurely walk towards Serenity's house. This was the kind of neighborhood that Patience used to live in. The lawns were landscaped. The windows had decorative shutters. The roofs were two and three stories high. Sidewalks ran along the streets connecting to driveways leading to garages. It sometimes seemed like too much space and too much property for two or three people. But, it was beautiful and what Fortune hoped to work for.

The faint music from the backyard of Serenity's party reached them along the way, guiding them towards the aroma of pizza, barbecue, and chicken wings in the air. They walked straight into the front door to find kids from school congregating in the living room and hallway in their perspective groups of friends. Fortune spotted Serenity by the stereo system with Chris and felt herself blush a little in embarrassment and envy.

She couldn't explain the feeling of self-consciousness she felt as she watched Serenity talk to Chris. She was completely at ease and confident in a black skirt and crop top. Her hair was pressed out with slight waves. Chris seemed to enjoy looking at her as much as he enjoyed talking to her. Fortune quickly turned away from the sight of the two of them and headed into the kitchen.

"I'm sure she's just being nice to him," Patience tried to encourage her as she picked up a can of soda and popped the top.

Fortune shrugged it off as she watched Miracle buzzing around the kitchen to make a fresh batch of fruit punch. "Who's being nice to who?" Miracle wanted to know.

"Serenity and Chris. They are in the living room talking."

"Oh..." Miracle's eyes widened and her mouth opened in the shape of a shocked circle. "I might have forgotten to explain to her that I invited him here to get to know you. I'll explain it to her when I see her."

"It doesn't really matter. Not if she likes him."

"Girl, you got dibs," Miracle assured her. "Girl code."

Fortune couldn't help smiling and feeling hopeful.

"Serenity got you working her party?" Patience asked jokingly as Miracle stirred the powder and sugar concoction.

"No, I just saw the punch was running low and that it needed to be done," Miracle commented.

"Is there anything in it?" Patience asked.

"There is water, punch mix, and sugar in it."

"Anything else?"

Anything like what?" Miracle asked confused.

"Hooch, booze, liquor... you know, hunch punch stuff."

"No. Serenity's dad is upstairs."

"Fine. Where's the food? I smell it, but I don't see any." Patience didn't hide her disappointment.

"Out in the back yard," Miracle told her as she filled two cups with ice and poured one for both of them. "Taste it and let me know what you think."

"Thank you," Fortune said as Patience took hers to the backyard in search of food.

"You're welcome," Miracle answered, before turning to find something else to help with.

Feeling a little on her own, Fortune decided to go back in the living room and see what Serenity and Chris were talking about. When she entered the living room they were both gone. She didn't want to imagine where. She strolled over to the stereo not sure what she was going to do or look at. She just didn't want to seem as alone as she felt at the moment. When she had made a cursory trip to the stereo and looked over a few of Serenity's photos on the wall, she turned back around, figuring that she could busy herself helping Miracle in the kitchen.

As she headed for the kitchen door, Chris entered the living room from the hallway and smiled at her.

"Hey Fortune," he said with a smooth smile. Chris was a pretty boy, which would usually be a strike against him. But he walked as if he knew he would own the world one day, and the way he played basketball made him a low-key celebrity at school. She certainly wasn't the only girl that took notice of him. So, she couldn't be mad at Serenity if she liked him too.

If she hadn't already been stunned by the closeness of her crush standing right in front of her, the fact that he knew her name wouldn't have been as lost on her.

"Hey Chris. I... My name is Fortune."

"Yeah, I know your name, girl." His eyes twinkled as he smiled showing off two rows of perfect teeth.

"You do?"

"Yeah, I've seen you with your girls at school. In fact, this is the first time I've ever seen you without them."

Fortune found herself at a loss for words. He knew her name and knew that she always hung around with her friends. The image of him talking with Serenity as they entered the party flashed in her mind.

"Oh, well... Yeah, I saw you talking with Serenity earlier," she began.

"Yeah, she came to talk to me when I first got here. I was asking Serenity about you. If she thought you might like me."

"You were?"

"Yeah, I thought maybe she could help me get your number."

"You did?"

"So, how about it?"

"Well, I don't know," Fortune was stunned to find herself replying. "I'd have to ask my dad first."

"Oh, you're a daddy's girl. I like that. I could ask him if you like."

"No, that's alright."

"Cool, so how about them digits?"

"Right," Fortune said, waking a little from the shock of her first encounter with him. "Just let me go get a pen and paper."

She could hardly feel her legs as she left him in the living room. She went into the kitchen to find Miracle and Serenity. Serenity sat on top of the counter next to the fridge nibbling on a large slice of pizza and sipping punch.

"Hey Fortune," Serenity said after swallowing her last bite. "I had no idea you liked Chris. I never would have tried talking to him if I'd known that. He—"

"He just asked me for my number," she blurted out and Serenity nearly choked as she gasped sharply.

"He did what?" Serenity asked when she cleared her throat.

"I couldn't believe that he knew my name and he said that he always sees me with you guys." Fortune felt her lightheartedness fade as she watched Serenity's face turn from three shades of yellow and pale to red. "He told me he asked you to get my number for him," Fortune relayed as she realized that he hadn't been telling the truth.

"That no good lying son of a..."

"He's a playa," Miracle put in.

Serenity smacked her hand on the counter before jumping down and heading out of the kitchen and into the living room. Fortune and Miracle looked at each other in silence until Serenity's voice was heard ringing loud and clear over everything else.

"Just who do you think you are, Christopher?"

They quickly followed her voice into the living room, both thinking that they would have to peel Serenity back from Chris. But they stopped short when they saw that he was standing next to another girl, frozen in the process of getting her phone number.

"You have got some nerve!" Serenity continued, yelling just above the music and getting the attention of everyone in the room. "How you gonna come up in my party, in my house, eat my food, then ask me and my girl for our numbers and then go after this girl when we're both out of the room?"

"What?" Chris asked as if confused.

"You not gonna play me and one of my best friends at the same time."

Fortune got a strange sense of satisfaction from watching Serenity shrink the basketball star down a size or two and his face glowed red from the embarrassment. "No, sir. Not here. Not tonight. Not tomorrow, or the next day, or next year or ever! Now, I suggest you leave my house before I go upstairs to tell my daddy to throw you out."

At the last threat, Chris's eyes grew wide with fear. The other girl snatched her number from his hand and he made a quick exit. With him gone, all eyes were on Serenity who seemed to become quickly embarrassed by her outburst.

"I am sorry you all had to see that. Please, enjoy the party," she said before she made a hasty exit up the stairs. Miracle and Fortune began to follow after but she held her hand up to indicate that she did not want to be followed.

"That was awesome!" Fortune heard a girl seated on the couch say. "Did you see his face? I always knew he was no good."

Fortune had seen his face, and she was glad that he got what he deserved. But, she'd also seen Serenity's face. Fortune wish she could have said all of those things to that boy. She admired the courage it took for Serenity to put him squarely in his place and kick him out. But, the look on her face once he was gone had matched the feeling Fortune had in her own gut. She felt foolish to have let him flatter her and make her believe that he was interested in her.

Like Serenity she had smiled up into his pretty boy face like an idiot, feeling overwhelmed by the fact that he even knew her name. And he had been confident in knowing what he was doing. He was the bad guy in the story but somehow, she felt as if it were her fault for not knowing like that girl on the couch that he was no good. She gave Serenity a moment to collect herself alone, then counted to ten and followed up the stairs after her. Careful of the carpeting, she took off her shoes and let her feet enjoy the soft plush feel as she took the stairs in her stocking feet wondering what it must be like having floors that were soft enough to sleep on. She took a short trip down the upstairs hallway, bypassing a bathroom that featured a large Jacuzzi tub and separate shower. It was not lost on her that her entire trailer could fit inside just the second floor and there would be room for more.

She was relieved to quickly find Serenity's door, decorated with her name and a poster of Pretty Ricky. She knocked softly on the door and heard Serenity calmly answer, telling her to come in. She opened the door to find herself in a room, decked out with the type of decorations, furniture, and accessories that Fortune could only dream about. Her full-sized bed with a shelf headboard and decorative footboard sat in the middle of a far wall with tables and lamps on both sides. An entertainment system with television connected to cable and stereo system connected to surround sound rested against the wall next to the door.

Serenity sat at a desk on a third wall stacked with her books and a laptop. She was wiping tears from her eyes, trying to clean up smeared makeup with a tissue.

"Are you alright?" Fortune asked her as she hugged her shoes to her chest self-consciously.

"No, I knew he was a player and I still got caught up in his stupid game."

"Don't blame yourself, he was pouring on the charm real thick down there."

"Yeah, but I knew that you liked him, too."

"Oh," Fortune said. "Well, then I guess I just dodged a bullet."

"You and me both," Serenity replied.

"You, me and probably half the girls at this damn party," Fortune joked.

Serenity's eyes widened in humor before she burst out laughing. "You know you right about that, girl."

Miracle and Patience entered at the sound of laughter and they all took seats around the room.

"I do not want to go back to that party," Serenity admitted. "I feel so stupid."

"Girl, don't give that boy the satisfaction of ruining your night. We are strong, beautiful, young, black women and we don't need no man!"

They all laughed again, and Fortune felt her spirits lift with Miracle's simple words.

"Serenity you live here, but your girls caught the bus and came way across town to party," Patience pointed out. "We gonna do just that."

Chapter Three: Beating the Odds

Fortune could feel the drain of a sixteen-hour day on her feet begin to seep into her bones. She gave the signal that she was ready to wrap it up and leave. Her publicist quickly announced that Fortune had a flight to catch, which wasn't true. There was just a car waiting for her in the parking garage to take her back to her hotel room. But, to suddenly announce that one of her best friends from childhood was in a coma was apparently not the best sound-bite to end a media reception. She was ushered from the room and then into the elevator that took her and her publicist down to the parking garage.

"You did good," Kim assured her as the elevator went down. "How are you feeling?"

"Just a little tired," she answered, not wanting to go into details about her sadness or speak about her dearest friend with the woman she'd worked with for more than five years but still hardly knew.

They rode in silence until the elevator door opened to the garage and they stepped out to a waiting town car and driver. A movement to the side caught Fortune's attention and she smiled through the rising tide of grief she continued to hold back to see Strength waiting for her.

"Go ahead and take the car," she told the publicist. "I have another ride waiting."

"I'm truly sorry about your friend," Kim replied, perhaps feeling the breadth of distance between them in the wake of Fortune's personal grief. "I'll put out a statement tomorrow and clear your schedule for the next two weeks."

She gave Fortune a friendly hug and saw to it that the bags she'd packed for her speaking tour were put into Strength's car. As Fortune approached Strength and the fierce

JAIRA B. WILLIAMS

hug of a true friend that awaited her, she thought back to her last year in high school, making plans for her future while working a part-time job that paid seven-fifty an hour.

***

"Who on Earth invented khaki pants?" Patience asked as she looked at her backside in the mirror near the department store dressing rooms.

"Why-pee-po…" Fortune whispered in a tone she thought would just be loud enough for Patience to hear. But she was wrong.

"Girl, you better watch your mouth if you don't wanna get fired," Miracle warned from behind the clothing rack.

"Fired from the Dress Bin. How would that look on a resume?" Patience teased.

"I think I'd have to skip that detail," Fortune reasoned. "Anyway, I don't think the pants we have to wear are anywhere near as bad as the shorts they wear down at Sporting Goods."

Patience nodded her agreement. "Yeah, but in both cases, you can tell that no person of color was in on the decision of professional attire for part-time work at the mall."

"Excuse me," a customer came up to the dressing area. "Is anyone working here? Can I get some customer service?"

"Sure," Miracle said, walking to the customer with a bright smile. "How may I help you?"

"I'm looking for a jacket for my daughter."

The customer pointed Miracle to a tall, slim, and awkward girl waiting by a rack. Fortune watched and listened as Miracle went over to help.

"What type of jacket are you looking for?" Miracle asked.

The girl shrugged.

"She's grown three inches in the last three months and I'm not sure if she's done growing. There isn't much in the Jr./Miss section that fits her. If she had her way, she'd wear jeans and t-shirts every day. But, she's a young lady, and I just want her to look her best. And I don't want to send her to school looking like a teacher."

Miracle beamed a kind smile at the young lady and Fortune noticed the girl was hiding in clothes that were too big and ill-fitting.

"So, what's your name?" Miracle asked.

"Tiana" she mumbled.

"Growth spurts are never fun, are they?" Miracle had an easy and instant connection with the girl.

"Come on, let's look around a bit and you let me know what outfits you like."

Taking Tiana around the store, Miracle made suggestions and the girl usually shook her head no. But, she managed to pull three outfits together that she seemed interested in and agreed to try on.

Miracle left them alone so Tiana could try the outfits, but Fortune noticed that she didn't go far so she could be on hand in case they needed anything else.

"Wow," she heard the mother breathe and walked to the dressing area to see the results. Tiana stood in the mirror turning in a slow circle as if she couldn't believe that it was her own reflection. "Honey, you are so beautiful," her mother said and the girl's smile seemed to stretch a mile wide.

"Girl, if you play your cards right you could be a model," Miracle said and the girl laughed.

She gave her a wink and left them alone after that, busying herself with straightening racks before the end of her shift.

"Thank you so much," the mother came up to Miracle. "She's going through that awkward phase."

"Oh, I know how that is," Miracle responded.

"Well, you are a miracle worker. I don't think she'd have believed me that she's beautiful but I think hearing it from you gave her ego a much-needed boost. Thank you."

"My pleasure," Miracle assured her.

Fortune couldn't shake the good feeling Miracle's attention to the girl gave her as she remembered how she'd done the same for her when they first met. Her phone buzzed her out of her nostalgia, reminding her that it was time to leave. She found Miracle to let her know that she was going.

"I need to clock out now and get on over to the school for Friday night school," Fortune let her know.

"You work too hard, girl," Miracle responded, surprising her.

"I have to," Fortune said, certain that the only way to be successful was to work as hard as possible.

"Alright, well... see you Monday at school," Miracle said.

Fortune took her father's car from the mall to the school because the bus schedule did not work out for the time frame she needed. She'd decided to double up on high school credits during the summer before her senior year into the fall so she'd have a light spring giving her more time to work and plan for life after graduation.

"You shouldn't work so hard, you're so young," her father had said one night while she plotted her schedule for the week. "You should be having fun. Have you even thought about Prom? Who are you gonna go with?"

"I don't know about Prom, Dad. But I have plenty of energy to do what I need to do," she assured him, even though at times it wasn't really the truth. "Besides, I want to buy us a mansion to live in before you're too feeble to enjoy it."

"Oh, you plan to move me into your fancy mansion, huh?"

"You know it. It's gonna be me and you, Dad. What do you think?"

"Yeah, that works for me," he replied with a thoughtful smile. "But, if you don't happen to make it to that mansion in time for me to enjoy it, I want you to know that I am extremely proud of you, baby girl."

"I'm proud of you too, Dad."

Fortune smiled wistfully, thinking about her dad as she drove across town to school. But every time she stopped at a light, her mind juggled a laundry list of things she needed to do for school over the weekend. She had to study for an Algebra test on Tuesday, work on her research paper for English due at the end of the month and prepare a Power Point presentation on current events for Social Studies. She could feel the pressure of trying to complete it all and still trying to work to save money pull in a knot at the bottom of her stomach. But, she could also see that almost everything that she ever wanted and worked for was just within reach.

She liked her night school class, US History. There was a lot of information to cover on the one night a week that the class met, but there was no real homework and only a series of quizzes as opposed to tests. Plus, the teacher was fun and entertaining, and it didn't hurt that he was cute. She took the front seat among her older classmates and opened her text and notebook. The subject of the class that night was the idea of Manifest Destiny. When the teacher entered the room, he divided the class into two teams to argue for and against the idea that the settlement of America was justifiable and inevitable.

"There is no such thing as destiny," one of the students in the class began. "The idea that there are forces or spirits that push us to a specific outcome is just a fantasy. I think the idea that America was inevitable just makes certain people feel better about how it came about. You know, the ends justify the means."

"How about you, Fortune?" the teacher turned his attention to her.

"Oh, I'm not sure if I believe in destiny. I don't think that anyone that works hard does. We work and then we are rewarded. I don't think that the ends always justify the means, but I do believe in hard work paying off. And if you work hard, in the end it's worth it."

***

Fortune thought back to the years of her life she dedicated to working hard in school and then in her career giving motivational speeches. She had meant so many times to take off and make time for her friends but there was always something to do and somewhere else she had to go, and she still didn't have a mansion. The cost of maintaining her public persona and employing a team to help with her image and scheduling was a financial burden. Not to mention the fact that she saw the three-story house that she did own in a gated community with a plush carpeting and marble counter tops only a little more often than she saw her friends.

"That was quite a speech you gave, Fortune."

After settling in the car and having the obligatory light and friendly catch up conversation, Fortune and Strength had remained silent for almost half an hour. She was jolted from her thoughts having forgotten that she was not in a car with a driver who only knew where to pick her up and drop her off.

"Thank you," Fortune replied softly smoothing a hand over the designer fabric of her pants. "But I guess I'm just a vessel."

"Oh..."

Fortune looked to Strength who wrinkled her nose skeptically. "What I mean is, the speech is inspired by His words."

"Yeah, I know."

Fortune could feel a sense of uncertainty and dread fill her heart. From the outside looking in, she knew that her rags to riches story was inspiring. She had in fact beaten the odds, worked herself to the bone, and left that trailer behind. But she hated to think of her speeches that were recycled and revamped on a quarterly basis. Deep down she knew—and possibly Strength knew it, too—that there was no love in her heart for what she did.

She'd spoken to Miracle a few times about her own business and the joy and enthusiasm she'd had over it had been enviable. There was a true and authentic light in the world so long as Miracle was in it. Fortune was certain that, if given a chance, she could make speeches for the next hundred years and not hold a candle to the true love Miracle had given out over the years. She never needed to charge people or be on a big stage to make others feel better about themselves.

Accepting

Why is it so hard for us to accept our struggles? A lot of the time you hear people say things like, "my struggles made me," but then why do we fight so hard to forget and not to re-live and accept?

I found out later in life that I had to appreciate my struggles, losses, and hurt by not just living with them, but through them, by healing, accepting and forgiving. It's easier said than done, but once it's done you'll be amazed at the inner and outer change in you.

Dear Genesis,

Childhood seems like so many lifetimes ago, doesn't it? I can't believe all of the things I've seen and done since those days. But I still think about and cherish all of the memories I have of us as kids. Including the first time I was able to go with you and your family to Holloway Gardens. How wonderful it was that your dad was the head chef there and could get us in for free. It was kind of them to let me come along and get us our own room together for a few days during Christmas vacation. I remember us sitting in the back of the car, riding through miles and miles of lights at Christmas time. It was so much like a magical fairy tale, wasn't it? I think maybe we can try and make it a new tradition. What do you think?

Or maybe we can try for an Easter spring tradition? I loved those weekends when your mother would just get in the mood to go there before it got too hot to enjoy the outdoors. The butterfly enclosure was my favorite spot, besides the pavilion cafe where we got to eat your dad's hot off the grill or straight from the oven lunch. I remember your mother sitting us down and telling us to be still and quiet so that the butterflies could land on us. I think that maybe one or two came near us. We couldn't sit still or quiet for long. But there were so many that surrounded your mother, dozens if not hundreds of beautifully colored butterflies landing on her dress, on her shoulders, and in her hair. It was like a dream, and I swear when I think back it was almost as if their tiny wings fluttered in slow motion making your mother seem like an angel. I don't think I would have been surprised if she sprouted her own wings to fly around the enclosure with them.

I know that you recently found out that your birth mom worked there as well. Have you connected with her? Now that we are older, we can see clearly all of the things about childhood that weren't perfect. But I hope that you see now that your childhood was really special and blessed with much more good than bad. I look forward to seeing and reconnecting with you soon.

Love,

Strength

FAITH

- *(noun) - complete trust or confidence in someone or something.*

Chapter One: Arrangements

As Faith opened the door to her office, she tried desperately to replace the image in her head of Miracle lying in the hospital unresponsive with an image of her full of life, spreading motivation and laughter personality. She'd been there at the end for so many of her clients and their families. She knew the prognosis was bad and in her mind, she prepared the same speech and presentation for herself. It would also be what the others would need to hear in order to begin letting Miracle go.

In the two years since taking over the funeral home, Faith Wright had yet to feel the same emotional hardship of making funeral arrangements and burying a customer as compared to when she buried her father. But even then, she'd had him to help her through the process and help her make the final decisions. That is the main reason she'd decided to become a funeral director in the first place. It seemed like a great way to help people going through one of the hardest times in their lives, laying a loved one to rest. She'd buried the earthly remains of bodies in every stage of life from babies born too soon to thrive to the elderly who'd wasted away after years of disease or neglect.

That day it was marked on her calendar to receive the remains of a young lady. The hearse would make its way to the hospital morgue at eight o'clock that morning and bring it to her mortuary. She remembered holding the mother of the young lady by the hand as she sat in the office and helped her leaf through images of caskets and liners. Her mother was one of the grieving that liked to talk about her daughter as if she were still alive. "She's gonna like this," she'd commented several times as she ran her hands over one of the fine satin options. The mother's tears had flowed freely, spilling silently as she turned her attention to the flowers she wanted displayed. "The hardest part was seeing her in so much pain," she'd remarked. "She's free from pain now."

Faith wondered who would be there to hold her hand and help her through this if she had to do the same for Miracle. It did seem as if she should be the strong one by default, but wasn't sure she could be. She'd known Miracle for a long time. It seemed as if it had been a lifetime ago, but at the same time, it seemed like it was only yesterday they were both making a bold transition in their lives. Miracle had just left the military and Faith was more than ready to move out on her own and into the world.

They'd officially met in class but hadn't become friends until they'd been connected through mutual friends that knew they both were apartment hunting. That is how they shared their first apartment together. In truth Miracle had done most of the hunting, being more than ready to move off of her cousin's couch in the middle of a living room that felt more and more like a fishbowl. Faith's father had been the first person to come see it when they'd decided that this apartment was the one. A loft sitting up high overlooking the Riverwalk, with two levels, high ceilings, and a huge kitchen with marble countertops. What more could she have asked for in her first place?

***

Faith had made a number of big adult choices in the summer following high school. She'd chosen to start working full-time right away and got a job as a cashier at The Marathon Mart. Her father insisted that she continue with her education. She enrolled and took classes at the community college part-time, figuring that she could work towards her associate's degree for two or three years before deciding whether or not to try for a four year degree. Miracle was in her first class and always had an interesting point of view during discussions, especially since she spent the last two years in the Army.

When they realized they were both looking for a place to live, they'd hung out together for a few weekends. They got along so well that they decided it would be worth a shot to look for an apartment together. Faith knew that she was ready to make this next step since she'd already navigated her first major purchase of a used car still in pristine condition, bought from a middle-aged woman who'd kept the eighty thousand mile car's oil change and service records in the glove compartment.

When Miracle found an apartment that she thought would be perfect for the both of them, she'd called Faith immediately and told her to hurry over. Miracle hadn't even waited for her to knock on the door. She dramatically flung it open with excitement and took Faith on a tour of the space, pointing out where they could put the furniture, dishes and accessories that they already had between them and what they would have to purchase together. They'd gone to the rental office and signed the lease together before anyone else could come and get it. Faith had been so excited to tell her dad all about the new place, and while he was surprised, she noticed his face turned serene and a little sad. He took a seat at the dining table and instructed Faith to take a seat as well.

"There is never going to be a good time to tell you this," he began gravely, and she felt the high of getting her first apartment begin to plunge.

"What's wrong?" she asked, wondering if she'd done something wrong.

"I haven't been feeling well lately. At first, I thought it was just a bug that would go away on its own. But, then... I noticed that it wasn't getting better and I went to get a check-up and have some blood work done."

Faith held her breath, waiting for him to relay that everything was clean.

"I'm sick," he explained. The tone of his voice left no room for misunderstanding. She knew right away that it wasn't something simple that medicine or surgery could cure. "Cancer," he confirmed after a small space of silence. "I may have six months to a year left. But God will have the last say."

Her father hired a moving company to take her things over to her new apartment and supervised to make sure they reassembled everything the way it needed to be. He went with her to the grocery store to make sure she had enough to eat in the fridge. When he was satisfied that everything was right and in its place he sat her down at her own table and unpacked a notebook of information that she would need for his funeral arrangements, just in case. Faith was struck by how the forms and pamphlets and booklets concerning death were so neat and tidy and even beautiful. "The doctor wants me to start chemotherapy next week. I'll need you to take me to the appointment and bring me home. Can you do that?"

"Of course," she declared, not knowing what that really meant.

He walked her through everything, and the funeral home director came to his home the next day to finalize the plans.

Walking into the treatment facility with her father, Faith got an eye-opening display of other patients in various stages of treatment. Most of the patients looked just as healthy as her dad appeared, strongly walking, talking and even laughing. She leaned closer to her dad. He squeezed her arm in understanding. There were some that moved just slow enough to indicate they were fighting an internal battle. Their glances in her direction were slow, registering mild interest in the new faces. The range of optimism she observed spanned from hope to hopelessness.

A nurse led them to her dad's treatment station, and she took a seat at his side. She watched anxiously as the nurse prepared his machine and medicine. She turned away as the nurse found a vein and stuck a needle in his arm.

Her eyes locked towards the floor until she heard the nurse say, "Alright, you're all set." She nodded her thanks to the nurse before she walked away, and then turned to her dad who seemed in good spirits. She handed him his book to read and began working on an assignment for school.

JAIRA B. WILLIAMS

The next few months became a slow blur of everything that she needed to do for school and work as well as what she had to get done to help her father through his illness. It was hard to think of a future without her dad. She tried hard to stay hopeful and talked positively whenever she was with him. Every day she woke up hoping that everything would just go back to normal.

But it never did. As her father got sicker, school quickly became a non-necessity and she found herself taking off more time than she had stored up in order to care for him. The last time she sat in the front passenger seat as he drove to church, he was a little tired but still in good spirits. He took his place as Deacon and did his part for the service as usual. He always looked so happy at church.

However, by the following week, the toll of the cancer and treatment had taken much of his strength. Now it was she that drove him to church, but he still found the strength to both sit and stand in the pew. The next Sunday when she came to get him, he was too weak to even get out of bed. It was not the first time he'd had to be rushed to the ER, but this time he didn't leave. After examining him, the doctor came to her with the option of hospice care.

"His organs are shutting down, and he's in a lot of pain," he told her.

She was surprised and confused but she made the decision to sign the papers so he wouldn't suffer. She worked quickly to finalize the last details for her father's funeral arrangements. He had made it clear to her that he wanted her to do it on her own and for no one to help her. Three days after signing him into hospice, she lost her father. With all the time she had taken off to care for him, she'd lost her job as well.

Chapter Two: A Funeral

Faith stepped into the back room of the mortuary where the young lady she'd received lay, just after being embalmed and in the midst of getting her hair and makeup done. Faith pulled an empty seat up near the young woman's side and touched her hand, already stiff, fixated by the formaldehyde. She took in the girl's features, lifeless and pale. There was no sign of the pain her mother had spoken of. But it had been like that for her father too. The last days especially, his features had been set in constant tension as if he were still trying to fight and will himself to live. If the prognosis was right, in less than a week it would be Miracle on the table. She was just not ready to face seeing Miracle like that.

Throughout her father's illness and after his death, Miracle had been the rock-solid constant in Faith's life. After her job loss, Miracle had to put more money towards the rent until Faith could get unemployment and food stamps. She had been the still, soft voice encouraging her every step of the way.

***

"I know you didn't know this was going to happen," Miracle would say whenever Faith felt the need to apologize for not being able to do more. "We're not on the street or starving, are we?"

"No, but I've had to file for unemployment twice already... I just don't like that."

"You know, you've got a lot of pride, and that's a good thing. But I know you just lost your daddy and only need help until you get back on your feet."

"Sometimes, it's like I don't even know which way is up or where my feet even are. If just one more thing happens... I just don't know what I'll do," Faith told her.

"You don't have to know. The Lord knows and He's already worked this and whatever comes next for you. If you ever want to talk about anything, you know I'm here for you."

"I know."

"If you want, you can tell me what's been on your mind."

Faith remained quiet for a moment, and then it was as if a dam broke in her heart and she finally put words to the thoughts and frustrations she'd held in since her father told her that he was sick.

"I imagined, all my life, of becoming an adult and at no point did I ever imagine he wouldn't be here. It just wasn't supposed to be like this, Miracle. I just don't feel like I had enough time with him. I feel cheated. I just always thought there would be time to ask him certain questions. I just wanted for him to see me graduate from college and succeed in life. I wanted to just get to know a little more about him. You know the things that he held back because I was too young to know. I mean, how many single dads take on raising a girl alone? That's something special, isn't it?"

"It sure is," Miracle agreed. "And I'm sure you know that it's because he loved you and he knew the best thing for you was to have him in your life."

"But maybe if he had left me with my grandma or other relatives... Maybe he could have been happier and done more with his life."

"He raised you because that is exactly what he wanted to do."

"He could get so angry sometimes, especially towards the end of high school. It was like his temper would come out of nowhere, he would just be so mean at times. I never really let it bother me but I couldn't understand where the anger was coming from."

Miracle listened calmly, then responded, "I am sure that all of the anger and frustrations were about him having to leave you alone. It just wasn't fair to either of you."

"And there was no time... It was like one day he tells me that he's sick and the next day I'm... I'm signing his life away to hospice care."

Saying the words out loud like that for the first time, *"signing his life away,"* hit her hard. He had been all she had, but she also had been all he had and there was nothing she could do for him. He was the father that had done his level best to give her everything and when he needed her, she couldn't help him.

It may not have been a fair way to view the circumstances, but she wished she had done more. She wished she could have done something. She hadn't even noticed that he was sick. How was it possible that he got down to six months to live and she hadn't even had a clue that he was ill? She'd been so intent on finding and apartment and she'd signed the lease so quickly. If she had known he was ill, she could have saved that rent money and put it towards caring for her father at home.

"Stop it," Miracle said forcefully. "Your father's journey came to an end and there was nothing you could do to change any of it. He is gone, Faith, so you have to let him go. You are still alive. As long as that is the case, a piece of him will always be alive with you. How do you think he would feel to hear you say those things? And what do you think he'd say to you in response?"

Faith had clamped her mouth shut at the thought. She wondered for a few moments what he might say, but she didn't answer Miracle out loud.

Chapter Three: All That You Can Be

Faith knew that she still had a small mountain of paperwork to do, but she could not overcome the need to help the mortician prepare the young lady for her casket presentation. As the hairdresser worked on combing and hot pressing the girl's hair, Faith rested a white towel beneath the girl's hands and then lifted a small bottle of pale pink nail polish from the supplies on the table. She lifted the girl's fingers and thumbs one by one until they were all painted with two coats, and then finished the look with a clear coat to produce a high gloss shine.

Faith lifted a slip which hung with the girl's favorite white dress on a clothing rack to the side. The mortician carefully held the girl's torso and placed her into a seated position as Faith pulled the slip over her. They worked together to shift her body to get it below her hips and settled just above the knees. They each took a leg and pulled up thigh high stockings and then worked again to maneuver the body into her white dress. Faith finished the ensemble with a pair of white slippers and the hair dresser moved in again to put the final touches of gel, hair pins and hair spray.

They all took a moment to look over everything to make sure it was done right. They smiled at each other nodding in agreement that it was perfect. They all seemed unable to leave the body alone, even as the beautician arrived to work on her makeup. The beautician was an elderly lady, at least seventy years old, but she worked quickly with the agility of her expertise, bringing just enough color to the girl's face to make it look as though she were sleeping peacefully.

As the body was finally lifted and placed into the coffin, Faith couldn't help but think of having to do the same for Miracle if she didn't recover. She couldn't help but feel the same way she had when it was time to put her father to rest. She just wished that she could have done so much more for Miracle to help repay her understanding and kindness when she lost her father.

***

Faith led the procession towards her father's casket in the pulpit of the church. She'd been apprehensive, remembering the graying pallor that took over his flesh in the hours after his spirit left his body. There had been a viewing in which she stayed the entire day: she was the first one there and the last to leave.

As she came to a stop by the casket, she took in the first of many small details, and decisions they'd made together. His tie was black with smoke grey stripes. Then her eyes traveled over his suit, dark grey and tailor-made with a smooth shine—he was always so detailed when picking out his suits. She looked to the other accessories, his gold cross necklace gleamed and hung so still around his neck, and though she couldn't see the shoes, she remembered they were his favorite church shoes, comfortable and well cared for. She thought back to seeing everything laid out on the bed just following his passing. She'd gone over the checklist three times before packing everything in a suit bag and tote for the funeral home. As she put the items away one by one it was as if his spirit were there with her, reassuring her for the first time that she would be okay and she could do this.

She had managed to get the suit to the mortician, but that was the least of the struggles that she would face over the following six months. She'd started job hunting the day after the funeral. It seemed to be harder and more pointless and still more urgent than when she first went job hunting. Her resume was short with only her part-time work during high school and her job as a cashier that she was fired from after less than a year. Then there was no way for her to get around explaining why she'd been let go and the conversation turning to the death of her father. It was exceedingly hard to convince hiring managers that less than a week after she'd buried her father, she was up to the challenge of getting back into the work force.

Every night she'd come home frustrated, wishing that she could just lay it out in real life terms. She was an orphan with no support or safety net. She had to feed herself, pay her rent, and cover her bills. She could swipe groceries, stock shelves and even flip burgers if she had to, just as well as anyone else and she felt she needed the money more than anyone else. But she'd never been able to make that speech.

It took two months for her to finally land a job as a Customer Service Rep for Daily Solutions Tax Company. Two months of scraping by, saving unemployment checks, and even the thought of selling plasma had crossed her mind. She'd taken a risk by letting her car insurance lapse. She was over the moon to find the job and settled into the new routine with a little breathing room and the ability to have a flowing income again. But, eight weeks later she was handed a notice that the company was going out of business and she was right back where she started.

Miracle looked more stunned and upset by the news than she had been. "There must be some type of severance," she'd said.

"Two weeks," Faith acknowledged. "So, I'll have enough for next month's rent but for the last two months of our lease, I'll have to borrow from family or file unemployment again."

Faith found it exceedingly hard to ask her relatives for money and not even have a guaranteed date to pay them back.

"You lost another job?" her grandma asked in disbelief.

"They are going out of business and I haven't had enough time to save much. I only need enough to cover two months, if you can spare it for a little while."

"Then what are you going to do for the third month, if you haven't found a job?"

"I'm going into the military," she announced and her grandma looked shocked.

"The military? Is that necessary? What about school?"

"I can't afford any of it on my own. They'll pay for school and I'll have a guaranteed check."

"Oh well, of course I can give you the money you need until then. And you won't even have to pay it back."

Faith had smiled gratefully as her grandma wrote her a check.

"Then I guess I'll need to get a new roommate," Miracle had said sadly when Faith told her of her plans. It had been a testament to how good a friend she'd been that she'd never even considered that Faith would have to move out. The last two months were still a struggle, but with the money from her grandma, prayer, and food stamps, she made it through.

Six months after that, she sent a check to her grandma of what she'd owed, and she gladly deposited the check.

Soul Search

In order for me to see God's full vision, I had to start healing. Meaning, reclaiming my energy from the daily drain of life and with that energy, start focusing on my peace. In that time my process began and those visions became clear.

Dear Genesis,

    I am sitting for a little while on my own out on the patio. The sun has set for the day and I have finally finished packing my bags. I'm going to stop by Fortune's presentation. I'm not sure if she'll want to see me, but I have a feeling that she'd rather drive to the hospital with me than fly there on her own or with her entourage. I am glad to see that she is doing so well. I get the feeling that sometimes she doesn't take the time to enjoy her own success.

    I don't know if you heard about Serenity's arrest. She ran into a little trouble. She's alright though. Patience went to pick her up and they are on the way to Faith's. Once I pick up Fortune, we'll head directly to Faith's and meet up with them before going to see Miracle in the hospital. But as I sit here looking into the darkened sky just over my backyard, I can admit to myself how hurt and lost I feel. I don't know how I'm supposed to come to a point of peace and acceptance. We just can't lose Miracle so suddenly. I think about these words over and over again: Death is a part of life, and we have to let go of what's already gone or else we will bury ourselves in our own hurt, pain and grief.

    I'm gonna try my best. That's all any of us can do. It's okay if you can't make it to the hospital. I will pass along your regards to the others. But, please do not feel as if you have to go through this alone. We all are praying she pulls through.

    Have you spoken more with your biological dad? Have you told him about Miracle? I hope that we can stay in touch.

Love Always,
Strength

DESTINY

- *(noun) - the events that will necessarily happen to a particular person or thing in the future.*

Chapter One: Guarded

Destiny Gordon opened the top dresser drawer where she kept her underclothes. The suitcase was already open on the bed, she just needed to find the will and focus to fill it with clothes. Hearing about Miracle was a punch in the gut that she would most likely never recover from. She closed the dresser drawer, not wanting to think about her in a coma, and took a seat at her laptop where her last post about Terrance sat prominently at the top of her social media feed.

"soul mate

/ˈsōl ˌmāt/

noun: a person ideally suited to another as a close friend or romantic partner."

"I've heard a soul mate cannot just be someone who you have relations with, but someone that you have a bond with, one that is unexplainable but understood between you two. A soul mate can come in the form of a friend, relationship or partner, not just in love. Life teaches us lessons we never realize until after the test. The universe and God align things and place people in your life for a reason, but it's up to us to see what that reason may be."

Destiny let her eyes scroll over the likes and past the comments on her post in order to see if he had acknowledged it himself. He hadn't. She wasn't too surprised. They'd broken up more than a year ago, and she'd just gotten back from deployment overseas. She'd thought maybe knowing she was back might spark something. She let her elbow rest on the table and wondered for the millionth time how a relationship that seemed so perfect in the beginning came to such an abrupt end.

***

"You never come out with us," Faith whined over the phone as she tried to get Destiny excited about a house party.

They'd joined the Army at the same time and stuck with each other; now, after three years of hard work they were both up for promotion from private to sergeant. It was Friday. She was a little tired, but Faith's excitement was contagious. So she took half an hour to shower and change for the party.

"I'm one to talk," Faith said as she drove and checked her lipstick in the rearview mirror. "I haven't been partying since the enlistment mixer. But there is something about being back home, isn't there?"

"Yeah," Destiny agreed, as she looked out towards the town that seemed to have stood completely still in the time that she'd been away. Nothing had changed. There was a certain level of comfort and sadness at the thought. The same people that were struggling three years ago with jobs and family problems were still doing the same things. She'd focused on getting to the military and it had paid off and she was doing well. She just wished that there was something she could do for others.

Faith seemed to feel the change of Destiny's mood as she suddenly turned the radio up full blast. "Draco" by Future played on the radio. Destiny turned her attention to Faith as she wiggled her hips in the seat to the beat of the music.

"You ain't got no kind of sense, do you?"

"Not when I'm about to party," Faith admitted.

They arrived at the party to find it was a little more low-key than she'd been expecting.

"Ok then, a chill party," Faith said, seeming as surprised as Destiny was. "I'll go grab the booze, I need a drink."

Destiny shook her head as Faith went inside and she strolled towards the backyard where a young man stood at the grill looking under tin foil and checking thermometers. She did a double take as she recognized him. She'd been wrong. Some things at home had changed. Terrance Coleman had gotten three years older and fine. She'd known him when she was still in middle school. She knew that he was older than her because when she'd met him he'd been friends with her older cousin in high school.

"You are taking this seriously," Destiny said, not sure if he'd remember her but still intrigued by his Master Chef routine.

"Yeah, a party ain't a party if the food ain't no good." He flashed her a smile that was a mixture of silliness and pride and she smiled back.

"I'm Destiny," she said, extending a hand.

"Yeah, Destiny, I remember you. No handshakes. Give me a hug."

"I remember you too, Terrance." She hugged him quickly and pulled back.

He smiled and she was certain that there was a slight blush as he nodded and looked her over, "That's what's up," he said as Faith made her way out of the house with two glasses of wine and handed her one.

"Hey Terrance," Faith called to him as she took Destiny by the arm and led her into the house. "I need a sipping buddy."

"Not unless we planning to stay over or Uber our way back home."

"Okay, party pooper. I got Uber on speed dial so there."

Destiny shook her head, agreeing that she should loosen up a little bit. In a few weeks she'd have more money in her paycheck and she needed to celebrate. Faith had a good time introducing her to old friends but was overwhelmed with emotion when Miracle showed up. They grabbed a fresh bottle of wine and the three of them spent time together playing cards and talking, allowing Miracle and Faith to catch up. Destiny didn't mind staying quiet as they wandered down memory lane. Miracle was quite a character and she'd been in the midst of writing a business plan for a new company she'd just formed.

"It's been one thing after the other, getting the paperwork filed and then finding suppliers and a way to drop ship that makes sense." She picked up her glass of wine and toasted to the air. "It'll be worth it though."

"Yeah, so when I get out of the military, you'll be able to hire me," Faith commented.

"You know what? That's the good thing about this kind of business. You won't need me to hire you 'cause you'll be able to set up your own shop."

"I guess I could own a business," Faith said thoughtfully. "But, for now it's me and Uncle Sam."

"So, what about you, Destiny?" Miracle asked.

"You know, I'm good for right now. Just getting to a place of being comfortable."

"I know right?" Faith chimed in.

"I'm just gonna kick back and relax. Just enjoy it for a while."

Miracle looked impressed and toasted the air again.

"Destiny, I think that dude is trying to get your attention," Miracle said and pointed behind her.

Destiny turned around to see Terrance headed towards her table with a tray piled high with food.

"What's all this?" she asked as he placed the tray in the middle of them.

"I know you were clowning my skills earlier. Just wanted to make sure you got a sample."

"Thanks, Terrance."

"'Sup ladies?" He asked her friends.

"This is a little more than a sample," Miracle pointed out.

"I know I gotta feed her girls, too."

"That's what's up," Faith said picking a piece of chicken from the plate and taking a bite. They all waited in anticipation and Faith nodded her head. "Yeah, your man can burn."

Destiny felt her cheeks flush but didn't think it would be appropriate to correct her. He wasn't her man.

"Well, I should get back to the grill," Terrance said, not correcting Faith either.

"Gurl!" Faith said around a mouthful of chicken. "You work fast."

"I ain't work nothin'," Destiny said, putting her playing cards to the side and picking up a piece of chicken. Miracle and Faith watched her like hawks, waiting until she finally nodded her head to confirm it was good.

"You should go tell him you like it," Miracle suggested.

"I'm sure he already knows how good it is. He's just being nice and besides he might have something going on already."

"Oh gurl please..." Miracle and Faith said at the same time.

That seemed to be enough to get them to change the subject and move back to playing cards. Not that she'd been looking for him to, but as the evening wore on into the night, she noted that Terrance didn't come back to get her opinion of his grilling. Enough time passed that Faith had completely sobered up and they went home without seeing him again.

It was a strange night for Destiny as she got ready for bed. She had meant what she said about being comfortable and just wanting to relax. She'd met all types of boys throughout high school, college and her years in the Army and had yet to find anyone that was her type. Besides that, she tended to be the shoulder other girls came to when this guy or that did them wrong. Still, she had to admit it had been a sweet and bold move to bring her a tray full of food in front of her friends.

She sat on the side of her bed for a moment. She had never done much dating. It had always been important for her to just guard her heart and stay in control. People come and go, that's the way it had been for most of her life, and falling in love for real was not something she was ready for. So, when he popped into her mind again, she said a quick but thorough prayer.

"You know Lord, I don't want to deal with any foolishness. But I don't want to reject something that might be good. I thank you for all that you have done, and all that you will do in my life. I just ask that you bring who is meant for me and you remove whoever isn't... no matter how good they are on the grill."

She was already in the bed when her phone chimed. She picked it up from the table and noted it was a text from her cousin.

"Gurl, why this boy blowing up my chat looking for you?"

"Who?"

"Terrance!"

Destiny nearly dropped the phone then texted back, *"I have no idea? What he say?"*

"Said you ghosted him at some party."

"I did not. I... I just left."

"Well, should I give him your chat name?"

"Yeah, alright."

But it wasn't until the next day that she got a message asking her out.

Chapter Two: Soul Mate

Destiny packed the last of her luggage and placed it by the front door. It had been three hours and not a peep from Terrance. It was still hard for her to think that maybe he just didn't care about her anymore. She thought about that night when she prayed for God to bring whoever was meant for her and remove whoever wasn't. She felt herself get angry and frustrated.

"Why you let me go through all of that?" she asked God. "If it wasn't meant to be, why you didn't just keep him away from me? It's not right. After everything..."

She let the rest of her complaints die out as she felt the spirit move over her. It wasn't exactly a peaceful feeling, but she realized that there were friends out there that did care for her. If he wasn't gonna say anything to her she should just rely on them. So, she turned back to her computer and posted about her friend. She wasn't surprised to find herself crying by the time she posted her prayers for and tribute to Miracle. She quickly got up from the computer and took her bags to the car. It was hard for her to do it on her own but she knew that she could because her friends were waiting in Atlanta.

She went back in the house to make sure that she had everything she wanted to take. As she sat at the computer to shut it down, she took note of the flood of messages and paused to see that one indeed came from Terrance.

***

It had been a low-key whirlwind of sweet and loving romance for six weeks starting with a date to get seafood and go to the movies. No one had ever taken up so much of her personal space before. It was a strange negotiation of changes that they both seemed to silently agree to. She appreciated little things that he paid attention to like the need for car washes and oil changes and how understanding he was around her during her time of the month. He surprised her on their two-month anniversary with reservations to travel to the beach in Pensacola, Florida.

The car ride was everything that she might have imagined taking a road trip with the right man would be. He'd even taken the time to put together a playlist that combined songs that they both enjoyed. It was also time well spent getting to know more about his mom and the rest of his family. She could imagine helping him pick out Mother's Day presents and visiting them for Fourth of July and Thanksgiving. It was exciting to think that her man came with a family that she might be able to call her own one day.

The waters of Pensacola Beach were a crystal blue that she'd only seen in pictures of the Caribbean or Hawaii. She could hardly believe that such a place existed so relatively close to them. After check-in, they took their bags to the twelfth floor and Destiny looked out over the beautiful and romantic setting, wondering how it was so that she'd gotten this lucky. They hadn't even bothered unpacking before putting on swimsuits and going down to the shore. They splashed in the water, bathed in the sun, ate the freshest seafood and became more intimate with each other than Destiny knew was even possible.

He'd presented her with a key to his house shortly after they returned from the beach, and she'd quickly returned the gesture. Everything about him and their being together felt right. She'd even used the word perfect on more than one occasion when telling her friends about him. For weeks they'd taken turns staying over at each other's place. She had made it a point to come home directly after work to prepare dinner, either cooking, heating-up leftovers, or ordering delivery. It seemed like there was never enough time for them to be together during the weekdays, between her work and school schedule and his long shifts. So they always spent his lunch breaks together.

Then one afternoon while preparing dinner for them at her apartment, he texted her saying he would be at his own place that night and not to worry about making dinner. She'd had half a mind to let him know it was too late and that he wasn't the only one she had made dinner for. She had to eat, even if he wasn't coming over. But instead she texted her understanding and that she hoped he was alright and that she would see him later in the week. That was the first night in months that she'd had to eat alone. The silence of the apartment was uncomfortable. There always seemed like something for them to talk about or discuss or plan for. She'd forced herself to make a plate, but her appetite had diminished to nearly nothing by the time she sat down to eat it. She missed him.

It was the same thing the next night and the night after that. After three days she'd begun to feel as if he'd ghosted her. Had his last call been his way of breaking up with her? There just seemed to be something exceedingly awkward and wrong about having a person next to you almost every day for four months straight and then gone.

"Did you have a fight?" Miracle asked when she described the situation.

"No, there was no fight or anything. I had come home for work and started making dinner 'cause the plan was to eat at my place. And you know... Not even a call. A damn text message."

"Have you called him?"

"No. Why should I call him? He's the one wanting space."

"So, you're just giving it to him."

"Exactly."

"For how long?"

"Not much longer. That boy gotta tell me something."

On the fourth day, she left work and went directly to his place. His car was in the driveway. She'd halfway been dreading seeing a strange car parked next to it. As she approached the door, she tried not to imagine him inside with another woman. But she had to know what was going on, knowing that it might break her heart. Even though she had a key, she rang the doorbell. He answered the door still in his work clothes and while he smiled and gave her a hug, she couldn't help but feel as if his smile was a little too small and his hug was a lot cooler than she'd been used to.

"I just wanted to come by and make sure you were alright, she quickly explained as she stepped in to look around. She could tell that he noticed her quick sweep of the surroundings.

"Yeah, I'm fine," he assured her. "I just needed some down time... on my own."

She nodded, not sure exactly what to say next or where to go from there. "Alright, well it has been almost a week, Terrance. I've given you space. I'm not sure how much more you're expecting or..."

She trailed off as he took a seat and looked at her expectantly. She was even more confused. She thought that would have prompted him to tell her what was going on, but he remained silent.

"I guess my next question is... Are *we* alright?" she finally asked.

"What do you mean?" The question pushed her very close to the last of her patience and understanding. How many different ways were there to understand that question?

"Don't act like you don't know what I mean. We been booed up for months now and all of a sudden... You need space. You don't even call to tell me you're not coming over. You send a text. The last thing I heard from you was a text four days ago. What is that? What is going on?"

"Yeah, well you tell me, Destiny. What is this? What is going on?"

"I asked you first."

"I asked you if we should get married before you leave, and you said no."

She felt as if a bucket of water had just been dumped in her lap as she remembered the conversation from the previous weekend. "I didn't say no. I said we should try and see what being apart for a year would be like for us, before we get married."

"Right," he said, as if there wasn't a difference between what she said and how he interpreted it. "And so right now I just need some time to myself to process that. Alone."

"That's not how relationships work. Nothing gets fixed if we don't talk."

"I don't need anything fixed, Destiny. I just need time to—

"Yeah, I get it. You wanna be alone. Later, Terrance."

She left the house with a strong urge to call him or turn around and try to fix whatever was broken between them, but she didn't. She went home quite certain that in a day or two she'd get a call driving the final nail in the coffin of their relationship. She held her tears in check until she finally got through her own door, and then she let them flow and she called Miracle.

"Am I crazy?" She asked after she'd explained the situation.

"No, he's probably all up in his feelings and don't know how to express them. He may really feel like you just rejected him or a marriage proposal."

"We've only been together a few months, Miracle, and then in six months I'm getting deployed overseas. Marriage is too much pressure, and is he gonna act like this every time he doesn't like what I say?"

"That's a very good question. If he does?"

"Girl!"

She didn't expect to hear Miracle laughing on the other end of the phone. But the laughter was so unexpected and funny that Destiny began to laugh too.

"So, I think now is the time to stop thinking about him and start thinking about you. If this is how he responds when you disagree with him, is that something you want to deal with? Married or not."

"I don't mind that he needs time on his own. I just don't like the feeling of being iced out. I mean, really?"

"That's something you will have to talk about with him. Write it in a letter and give it to him if you feel like you want this relationship to continue."

Destiny felt better after talking with Miracle, who seemed to have all the right answers. She'd sat down at the table and wrote a letter. In fact, she wrote three of them, but he never saw them. He turned up at her house out of the blue that weekend with a bouquet of roses and take out. She had missed him. And seeing him again, the last thing she wanted to do was push him away with the heated words she'd written down days ago. She just wanted to forgive, forget and move forward. Until it happened again.

A text to say that he wasn't coming over and not to worry about dinner for him. Well, at least he understood she still needed to eat without him. But she texted back that she was on her way to his place. She wasn't gonna wait this one out.

"Hey," he said, sounding a little surprised that she'd let herself in with the key that he gave her. True, she'd never had to use it before, but they'd been together for six months. It shouldn't have been a shocker.

"What did I do this time?" She asked trying to remain calm.

"What do you mean?"

"Well, last time you shut down on me, you said you needed space."

"Maybe my mood has nothing to do with you this time."

"Maybe you should find a better way to communicate your feelings to me."

"I'm feeling like I need to be alone."

"Why?"

"I can't communicate how I feel without having to explain every little detail?"

"You just want me to leave?"

"Yes."

Again, she got the feeling like someone dropped a bucket of water in her lap. "Got it."

She left the house placing his key on the counter. When she got back to her place, she cried of course and then prayed for God to heal her heart and help her understand. He never returned her key, but she left a box of his things on the porch for him to pick up.

Chapter Three: Heartbreak

It took every ounce of strength she had not to immediately reply to his message of encouragement. Over the last year she had of course heard that he'd been seeing other people and she'd run across some occasional post on social media of him. There had been a sliver of hope that after she got back they might be able to reconcile, talk things over, and try again.

As she looked at his post, she wondered if this could be that opening. But, she hesitated taking the time to really think about whether or not that was what she really wanted. Life had consistently taught her that people come and people go. She could count on one hand the number of people she met after high school that she stayed in constant contact with. But, she had been alright with that. Everyone still in her life were people that she wanted around. Most people were easy to let go of, but Terrance was not one of those people.

***

Destiny spent the weeks leading up to her assignment in Korea keeping busy with work, packing, and getting her house ready for renters while she was away. Adjusting to eating alone was a challenge, but sleeping alone was nearly impossible at first. She'd wake up several times a night to the empty space beside her and the quiet apartment around her. She hired a company to move her furniture into storage and left a few valuables and electronics with friends and family.

Travel to Korea took forever. It might not have bothered her or been so bad if she'd been able to think about anything else other than Terrance and what really went wrong in their relationship. She'd known that he was in a mood when she dropped by his house. She had not wanted to get into it with him. He'd known how much shutting down and icing her out had hurt her feelings the first time he did it. She hadn't given him her letters, but she'd found a way to let him know her thoughts about communicating. He seemed to have understood.

"I'm not a mind reader." She'd had to tell him that more than once, even when he hadn't completely shut down on her. "You gotta tell me what's going on in your mind or else I'll worry, and I'll not know what to do."

"Yeah, you like to fix things and make people happy," he'd said. "I know that. But baby, I want you to know that I just need to be by myself sometimes. I've always been like that. I'm not really used to having to tell someone when I want to be alone."

"I'm not used to a lot of things about being in a relationship. But, I adjust. I just want you to try and adjust just a little for me."

She understood what he said. But in a way it wasn't just that he wanted to be alone. It was that he didn't want to be with her as much as she wanted to be with him and the thought of that was painful. She'd let him in and he'd been like the sun bringing warmth and happiness. So, when he was gone, he took that joy and sunshine with him and there was no way for her to fill that space until he came back again. It really wasn't fair to her. The only way he could feel better was by making her feel alone.

She'd had to excuse herself to the bathroom more than once on that trip over to let herself cry and pray for healing. The same thoughts swirled around in her mind for hours until she considered that maybe he really didn't know how much leaving her alone like that, even for a few days hurt. But, how could he not know? He should have known. If he really loved her as much as he'd shown, he would have known. She'd fallen asleep at some point over the Pacific Ocean and of course her dreams were a continuation of those thoughts, only if she was able to talk to him in her dream and he was able to tell her everything that she wanted and needed to hear. Primarily "*I'm sorry.*"

When she finally landed in Korea, she didn't have much to do before checking into her unit, so she met up with other early arrivals and they decided to check out the city of Seoul. The culture shock alone was enough to take her mind away from obsessing over Terrance and what went wrong. Everything was foreign and needed negotiating: the cars, the signs, the money, etc., but they made their way through Yongsan where she picked up a few trinkets for people back home. They ended the evening in a small café run by a couple with their three children that could not have been older than teenagers. That is when her thoughts fell back to Terrance and the family, she'd imagined having with him. Why had she decided to just drop by his house when he texted that he wanted to be alone? If she hadn't done that... Maybe they would still be together. Maybe they would have been able to work through their differences.

Her mood saddened considerably, but she didn't want to show it to the others. She kept a smile on her face and faked her way through the rest of the evening until she got back to her room where she found herself too jet lagged to cry and quickly fell asleep. For the first time since the breakup, she just allowed herself to accept that she was alone. Really alone. Not only was that sad, it was also scary, because she really didn't think that she could ever let anyone else get close to her, not the way she had with Terrance.

She woke up in the middle of the night and started putting away her luggage and setting up her laptop. She'd uploaded pictures she took while out on social media and was surprised by the number of likes and comments which included well wishes from a few of Terrance's family members. She didn't know what to think about that as she scrolled through, but she saw more than a few comments from Miracle and decided to text her back and get her thoughts on it.

"I wouldn't read too much into it. They are good people, but I would think that it's a message from them and nothing more."

Destiny tried to take the advice to heart, but when she caught sight of a post about him with someone else, she knew that there was a lot of work that she'd have to do to get over him, and again she turned to Miracle.

"So, what do you think you could have done differently?"

"I guess not be so impulsive and more understanding."

"I think that you completely understand now that he wanted to have his own space. Right?"

"Yeah..."

"So, he's probably always gonna want his own space. And that is always gonna leave you feeling some kind of way. You know you can't wait around two or three days for him to decide to grace you with his presence."

"But... Why not?" Destiny wondered. She had lived her whole life before him without him. What were two or three days every few months? That's really nothing. It's not like she didn't have other things to keep her occupied.

"You tell me," Miracle responded. That is when Destiny understood what kind of work she needed to do in herself. It shouldn't feel like someone brought the sun with them. Yes, she should want to be with him and he with her but... when he shut down and iced her out, it felt as if she were stuck waiting and unable to move forward. She had seen herself married to him. Maybe not before leaving for a year. But she had seen herself with him and possibly getting married once she got back. His constant presence was a reassurance that a future for them was going to happen. His absence made that future seem less and less certain.

"I don't know," she finally responded to Miracle. *"But it shouldn't feel like that."*

As she worked more on understanding herself, Miracle became a good person, and basically the only person to tell her thoughts and reflections to. After a while Terrance became less a topic of conversation and Miracle began to share information on how her business was doing. She picked up on the gist of it and became more and more interested in how to start her own company.

***

Destiny looked at the message from Terrance. There was so much that she wanted to say and share with him. Mainly how much she had grown and changed in the time since they broke up, some new ideas she had, and to just laugh how they used to. But she stopped herself and powered down her laptop. It could wait until she got back.

Shifting

To change, especially unpredictably.

When I speak of shifting it makes my heart smile, it fills me with uncontrollable joy, and it gives me the sense of feeling complete in that moment. When I speak of shifting, I start with how my mindset changed, my thought process and how I completely broke my life down and relived it piece by piece.

I did that until it formed me into my master-peace. I smile as I speak of shifting because it is more than unpredictable, it is life-changing, life-gaining , hell, it's amazing! The things I went through to get here… I would do it all over again, because everything happens for a reason, and if those things don't happen how can we get to that shifting point?

Feel it in every word. Your mind isn't playing tricks on you; God did it and the Shift feels like New Life.

MIRACLE

- *(noun) - a surprising and welcome event that is not explicable by natural or scientific laws and is therefore considered to be the work of a divine agency*
- *A highly improbable or extraordinary event, development, or accomplishment that brings very welcome consequences.*

Chapter One: Miracle, Inc.

With no other options, Miracle walks into the mall recruitment office to look into what the military can offer her. The recruiter, a good-looking man with a smart and crisp uniform spins a great tale about the adventure, the travel, the career training, and of course the money. It seems like a great opportunity and she signs right away. She lands at basic training and spends two and a half months learning to be the best soldier she can be. Maybe basic training is easier for her than most others because she's already faced and overcome so much hurt and disappointment in her life. However, she isn't prepared for the competitive nature of the organization. Especially having to compete with men. She isn't expected to do better than them, so when she is better, she is also isolated. There is a balancing act to being in the military, and it pushes her away from forming any real relationships. Even when she does try, she finds herself consistently choosing to focus on her career in the military and being unhappy in her personal life.

When it's time to re-enlist she thinks long and hard about whether she can play that balancing act for another four years. She's a woman who is not expected to do better than her male counterparts and is also barred from certain opportunities. In addition, she was often judged by her skin color, weight, body type, and even the texture of her hair, causing unnecessary strain above that of her already stressful military life. And the money isn't enough. She decides that she can do it all again for another four years, but she doesn't want to. She's saved a lot of money from the last four years and decides to move in with her cousin for a few weeks until she can find an apartment, enroll in college to take classes, and get a part-time job.

She is fortunate to find a work-study job on campus and an apartment not far away from that. However, there is so much time on her hands that she has not had before outside of school or work, there is no place to be and nothing to do. So she is isolated again in a world of college students her age being upperclassmen and those she shares a class with being younger. She experiences a new and very real type of isolation and it is scary.

"I need to do something with myself," she tells Fortune when they meet up for lunch.

"What do you mean? You served your country for four years and now you are getting an education."

"I don't know. Maybe I just really missed the boat for college. I've seen so much of the world and was so active but now I just feel mostly like a bump on a log."

"You know what you need? Another you to tell you how amazing you are and that you are definitely being way too hard on yourself."

"Another me?"

"Girl, don't you remember when we were in high school working part-time. You made customers feel so good about themselves, no matter what it was they needed."

"It was my job."

"If that's the case, it was my job too and I completely sucked at it. Everything I'm writing in my book right now comes so natural to you. I'm almost jealous."

"But, that's just who I am..."

"Of course it is. Is it possible to just make who you are a career?"

"Yeah, sure. I'll just call it Miracle, Inc.. Everything is twenty-nine dollars and ninety-five cents."

"I love the name for sure," Fortune tells her.

Miracle gets ready for bed that night, turning the idea of starting a business over and over again in her mind. She takes a seat at her computer and Googles the meaning of the name Miracle.

"Miracle - a surprising and welcome event that is not explicable by natural or scientific laws and is therefore considered to be the work of a divine agency."

"Well why the hell not?" she finally asks herself.

***

Three years later, Miracle wakes to the brisk chill of winter and moves quickly from her bed to pull on her running clothes, socks and shoes. It is just before sunrise, as she steps out of her apartment into the chilly air to begin her two-mile jog, a routine she has kept up since her time in the Army. She remembers those times as she enjoys the feel of the cool air in her lungs and bounces from side-to-side to warm up her body and then stretch her arms and legs. She starts on her jog as the sun's rays spill over the horizon and light up her path. "One foot in front of the other," she reminds herself, as the first few minutes of the run are always the hardest.

She pushes herself past thoughts of stopping to walk or returning to the apartment and getting back in bed for another thirty minutes of sleep. Five minutes out feels much like the point of no return. Once she reaches that, her body is adjusted to the rhythm her feet make on the pavement. All thoughts of the creature comforts of home fade away and she turns to the first words of self-love for the day.

"I am a work of divine agency. God placed me here with a purpose and I choose to walk in that purpose," she thinks as she turns from the sidewalk onto a running path through the park.

Her legs burn a little as she begins the slow incline of the path that would last another two minutes. To take her mind from the pain she contemplates what it must mean to be a work of divine agency. She lets her mind travel back to her early childhood, through her time in school and her career in the military. She allows herself to recognize the pain in her past, every cut that still hurts but also makes her stronger, as she feels her legs burn every step until the pavement finally plateaus. She's running on level ground once again and realizes that the morning run is already half over.

She makes it to the first turn that will take her back to the sidewalk and begins a mental checklist of everything she must do that day. She has ten orders to fill, package, and ship. Then she must head across town for a speaking engagement followed by setting up a vending space at an expo business event. After that she has a meeting at a bank to apply for a business loan to help her with her finances and hopefully get a storefront location. She knows the chances of her getting approved at this point are not high, but at least she'll learn what she needs to do and how long it is going to take.

She gets back to her apartment energized from the run and ready to do what she needs to do. She steps into the apartment, still chilly and heads to the shower to get washed up and stay warm. There are many things Miracle sacrifices to help keep her business afloat especially since Faith had to move out. Overnight and early morning heating is one of them. It isn't freezing, not yet. She hopes that the weather will stay bearable until she is able to fill her Christmas orders. As she soaks up the heat of the shower, her thoughts briefly turn to the fact that she doesn't have a partner. Not in business or in love. The feeling of bitter loneliness hits her for a moment, but she banishes it with promises of a better future. She takes her time drying off in the heat of the bathroom and swipes a dab of liquid soap over the mirror to clear off the fog. The morning routine is the same every day, shower, brush teeth, apply makeup, and get dressed.

The cold of her apartment isn't so bad after she's dressed and ready to leave. She pours a cup of coffee, set to a timer every morning and takes a seat at the table to look over her current and past due bills. It has never been this bad, Miracle realizes as she looks at her bank balance in comparison to what's due and feels an overwhelming sense of pressure. She feels a slight tightening in her chest and takes several steadying breaths. She finishes her coffee and sits up straight in her chair. Closing her eyes to the reality of the bills and her bank balance, she silently reminds herself of the Christmas orders that she will fill and how everything would look completely different before Christmas. However, the reminder of Christmas underscores the fact that she is alone and doesn't really have anyone to share it with.

"It's lonely at the top," Destiny jokes with her one night on a call from Korea. "But you're doing great things and it won't always be like that. We're all busy this year but by this time next year, Faith and I will be back in the states, Fortune will be done with her speaking tour, Patience will have her law degree and we'll make Strength and Serenity take a real vacation for once."

"It's lonely," Miracle admits.

"Well, then tell me why do you do it?" Destiny asks her.

"I love helping people feel better... better about themselves and their lives and everything."

"Okay, so what would you tell someone in your same exact position?"

"I would say to be honest about what bothers them, and then to meditate on what is positive and focus on manifesting the life they really want."

"There you go."

It is hard for Miracle to admit, even to herself, that what she really wants, besides a successful business, is to have a partner in her business and in life. In the middle of the night, after a day being the best person she can be and working as hard as she can, she doesn't understand why she isn't enough for someone to decide to take a chance on her. She couldn't even remember the last time anyone asked her to go out and just have a meal or enjoy a concert.

Chapter Two: A Realization of Shifting

Miracle packs her car with inventory to display for various vending events throughout the early spring. She thinks about being rejected for her business loan for the third time and wonders if she is in way over her own head with this business. It is hard to stay positive in the face of rejection by the bank, especially since she is sure her business model and projections are great.

She gets to the first location, a downtown Farmers' Market made up of mostly local businesses and farmers. The revenue she achieved from her Christmas sales are enough to keep her company afloat through the summer. She made strides with a few local storefronts and boutique shops in the months leading up to Valentine's Day and is looking forward to the orders that will come in for Mother's Day. If she does as well for Mother's Day as Christmas, she will be able to breathe a lot better and keep the heat on throughout the night all winter long. Her strategy involves committing to vending opportunities and taking on speaking engagements in order to build-up her e-mail list and boost her online clientele and sales.

As she sets up her booth at the Farmers' Market, she takes note of a few other small business owners that she's met at other local events and they wave to each other. The foot traffic starts off strong. Miracle is proud of the sales, the list of new e-mail addresses and several business cards she's collected before lunch. When things slow down, Dria, who set up a booth for her nail salon, takes a break to speak with Miracle.

"Hey, girl!" she says after they hug.

Miracle picks out two bottled waters from her cooler and hands one over.

"Last I talked to you, you were interested in applying for a loan through your bank. How did that go?"

"It didn't," Miracle admits. "Three times."

"Oh, I am sorry to hear that. I know that cash flow makes a difference. But, you seem to be doing alright."

"Yeah, you know, I'm good. I just can't seem to see more than six months ahead."

"Have you tried the Small Business Administration? They have several small business loans and even some grants for black and women owned companies."

"I had heard about that. I will look into that next."

"It's how I got my startup funds for the salon. Speaking of which, we sold out of your care packages and will need some more."

"That's good to hear," Miracle smiles, but still something doesn't feel right.

"What is the matter?" Dria asks her when a pause lasts just a little too long.

"I don't know," Miracle admits. "Is it even worth it?"

"Owning your own business? Of course. You wanna punch in and out for someone else?"

"Nah, I can't see myself doing that... ever."

"So, what's got you down?"

"I guess I was expecting to have some kind of company with people, you know? Like you. Not be all by myself."

"You have to remember that I started my business over a decade ago. And I had my husband's day job for support. It's going to be a little bit harder but I am too proud of you, standing on your own and doing it girl!"

Miracle nods. "I guess I am."

"One thing that helped me in the early days, was actually reading about other people. How they got started and some of the challenges they faced. I will send you a list of books, most of them are audio so you can listen when you're home or on your morning jog."

"That's a good idea," Miracle says, feeling a little bit better. "I guess the kicker is really that I don't have anyone to share it with either."

"Not yet," Dria says before taking a look out to a new crowd coming in for the lunch rush. "Don't worry about having some significant other. When the time is right, that will fall into place as well. Also, be careful what you ask for... men come into our lives needing just as much love and support as we need ourselves. Are you ready for that?"

Miracle finishes her spring vending tour with a massive list of audio books to listen to beginning with Michelle Obama's "Becoming" and Stacey Abrams' "Lead from the Outside." The list continues with people and titles she's never heard of such as "Zero to One" and "Never Eat Alone." In the weeks leading up to Mother's Day she listens to "Red Ocean Strategy", "Blue Ocean Shifts" and "Purple Cow Transformations" and was the first to download Fortune's audio book "The Challenges of Life". She even deviates from business and self-help titles on her list into spiritual and wellness books.

While filling her Mother's Day orders, she comes to the end of Fortune's book and it finally dawns on Miracle that listening to all those books, by people she's never met somehow eliminates her feeling of being alone. She realizes in a new way how much she is a part of something greater and more important than just having a spouse. She is making a difference. She hears this all the time every day from her clients, and customers. She even has a page full of grateful and appreciative feedback on her website. Being a work of divine agency takes on a deeper meaning than it ever has. She doesn't have a significant other, but plays a small part in significant moments for countless others.

She also begins to admit the fact that she doesn't have someone special in her life may be because she was not ready to let go of feeling hurt. She doesn't want to get hurt again and she is closed off. She had chosen her career over the men she dated, but none of them had thought she was worth the compromise it would take to be with her and also allow her to be successful in the army.

Finally, she realizes that holding onto the hurt also forces her to hold onto the fear that if she does open up to another love, she will have to choose between that person and her business. She would never be able to do that, so she closes herself off to avoid facing the choice at all.

Chapter Three: At Peace

"It is an understandable rationalization," Fortune tells Miracle on one of their late night/early morning phone calls. Fortune was on the other side of the country addressing a conference about the topics in her new book.

"It might be understandable, but it isn't healthy. I cut myself off from love on purpose because the guy might feel neglected by the time I put in my business. That is a little messed up."

"Yes, you're right it's not a healthy way of thinking. But don't be too hard on yourself. Relationships take work. And I think that it is okay to put yourself into the shoes of the other person that would have to put up with your business schedule."

"I do understand that from a business perspective, but I want someone in my life. I want both. Can't I have both?" Miracle knows that it is an impossible question for Fortune to answer.

Her business is doing well. And she's just been approved for an SBA loan that gives her the financial backing she needs to move into her own storefront space. It is a big move and an intimidating one too. When she walks into the storefront space for the first time as its owner, she is overjoyed beyond words to finally see her dream in the real world. She'd taken her business plan to the SBA and they'd given pointers on what she needed to improve. However, because she is a woman and a minority, she got an approval on her first application.

She spends two weekends buying furniture, decor and accessories and then moving her current inventory from the guest room in her apartment to the floor space of the store. In all she, puts together over four hundred self-care, encouraging, and inspirational packages. Giving each one a special touch and message that she herself needs to from time-to-time hear. When she feels herself becoming overwhelmed, she dedicates a space in the store to meditate, reflect, and recharge. On her morning runs, she allows her spirit to reach out and take in messages of love and healing that she listens to on audiobooks, TED Talks, or podcasts. It is wonderful to have a loan, but as the second week came to a close, she gets her first notice and feels the pressure of having to begin paying that loan back.   When everything is in the perfect place, Miracle hires a local PR company to announce the launch of the first Miracle, Inc. store location.

"I am so excited for you! I wish I could come back just for that," Destiny says on a call with Miracle just before the grand opening.

"I wish you could, too. But, you sound like you're adjusting a lot better in Korea now."

"I think I am," Destiny agrees.

"Did you meet someone new?"

"Oh no, girl. I ain't got time for that out here. No, I decided a little while ago to think differently about Terrance."

"Okay. How so?"

"Yeah. The heartbreak was a little devastating. But, I had to start being honest about some of my own part in it. I mean, I think of it like this now. Every experience in my life adds a new puzzle piece to who I am as a person. And my experience with Terrance added a new piece to my puzzle, you know giving me more information on who I am as a person and who I need in a boyfriend and husband. I mean, I'm never gonna accept a man that handles his problems by avoiding difficult feelings and not communicating. I know that about myself and know Terrance, at least for right now, is a guy that shuts people out when he wants his own space. I want him to be happy. But, I want me to be happy more."

Destiny chuckles a little and Miracle nods in response to her new point of view on her breakup.

Miracle took half an hour before going to bed to pull out a piece of paper and try it Destiny's way. What were her faults?

I have a temper... and I'm a little selfish.

"But that shouldn't really matter because I'm also extremely generous," she argues out loud and then realizes that she is expecting others to overlook her faults because of her good deeds. She takes the time to unpack that, listing three instances where she may have been a little selfish in her relationships.

Sometimes, I feel like a victim of things that have happened to me.

"That sucks because I feel like there is nothing I can do. I don't like feeling like that. But, I'm not sure how to change that." It is frightening to face this realization, but she also feels as if the admission is freeing and a turning point.

I need to forgive everyone I think hurt me.

She knows that one will take some time. There is so much disappointment that she is still holding on to. But, holding on to it and thinking on it is taking a lot away from her positive energy. She wants to be happy and not being able to forgive is stopping that.

I have to stop seeing my mistakes as mistakes.

She has known for some time that this is a problem for her. A side effect of being in the military, wanting everything to be perfect and "high speed" sometimes stops her from enjoying most of her successes when a few things go wrong. She needs to focus on viewing whatever goes wrong as experiences to learn from and should find ways to celebrate on her own more of the little things that go right without obsessing on things that go wrong.

She goes to bed truly hopeful that changing her way of thinking will lead to her being happy. She wakes up the following morning and gets ready to face the store's opening day. She is blown away by the response from customers that bought out her inventory in the first two weeks.

"Hey, Strength!" She answers her cell phone at the end of those two weeks.

"I tried to place an order on your website today and saw that just about everything is on back order."

"I still have a few things in the closet. What did you want to get?"

"I'll take whatever you got left. Congratulations by the way!"

"Thank you!"

"How does it feel?"

"It feels good, Strength. It feels really good."

Destination

What are your plans? Did you write them down? We hold most of our thoughts, goals and ideas inside because we fear they won't reach the level we desire. Let's change that!
We can't hold back what has been placed on us out of fear of rejection or duplication of what someone else is doing.

> Visualize it
> Write it down
> Put in the work and
> "Make Your Visions Visible."
> -   Jaira B.

STRENGTH

- *(noun)* - *the quality or state of being strong, in particular. A good or beneficial quality or attribute of a person or thing.*

Letter to Myself

In my life, I have ignored so many signs and so very many lessons. Not too long ago I woke up one day to realize that I'd strayed so far away from my truth. So far away, in fact, that I didn't even know what my truth even was anymore. I had to start with trying to define it for myself: just what is *my* truth exactly? I decided that my specific truth is made up of the things that have been placed in my life to help me grow, to teach me. Unfortunately, that means my truth can sometimes even hurt me. In the past when life's lessons hurt me, I just pushed them to the back of my mind. If I didn't think about it, if I could just forget about it, then I could get past it. But, now I know, I couldn't ignore the pain forever, and certainly couldn't forget. I simply set it all aside temporarily until there came a day, a reckoning, when I had to work towards my truth and I becoming one.

As the years go by, life will throw one thing and then the next towards us. We are adults, so we handle one thing and then the next. And the next. And then the next. More years go by, and life's hurdles seem to get higher and higher. But actually, the hurdles don't get higher, it's just that the weight of everything we thought we dodged or got past gets heavier and heavier. And it gets to the point that if just one more thing happens... No, not *if* one more thing happens, but when. When one more thing happens, and life decides to throw even just a little more than we can handle, we then realize our "breaking point," as we call it. But really, we've finally climbed to the foundation of our healing stage.

It is at this stage that we have a choice. We can choose to keep ignoring all of life's lessons or we can see that this is the realization stage in life, where we can go back and learn to accept what we've been ignoring. We stop ignoring the pain that we've come through. We can stop avoiding it and we can actually embrace it. It's a scary prospect. But, how can we learn the lessons that we're supposed to if we are not even willing to acknowledge them (and the pain they've caused) from the start?

In my acknowledgment of everything I've been carrying around, I wrote letters to myself or rather to my beginning self. I wrote to the adolescent me, the me who thought life was going to be perfect. In the beginning of my life, everything was great in my eyes. I dreamed so much about what my life would be like when I grew up. I dreamt about being on TV shows, cooking, acting and so many more achievements. I was able to dream this way because my childhood was pure bliss. My mom owned her own hair salon with my aunts and grandmother. My dad worked as a chef, football and basketball coach, and a few other hustles (if you catch my drift). We took vacations often and we traveled during the summer. My mom was truly a sweet angel and my dad was my OG, as I call him. He knew so much about life and although he was hard on me sometimes, everything that he was, everything that he said, everything that he did, it all made sense in the end.

The first challenge, or hurdle in life I faced, I remember that being the day my dad took me for a ride and told me that I was adopted. I know right, how ironic? I honestly don't remember feeling any emotion; it never made a difference to me. It was truly like a movie. In one breath he told me that I was adopted and it seemed as if in the very next he told me how my biological mom tried to take me. Shocking, right? I loved my life the way it was and wanted nothing to change. See that's another thing about me back then: I hated change. I didn't like to move. I didn't like to change schools or anything that took me out of my comfort zone. But something had changed. I knew something new and different about myself. I didn't let it bother me, though. My dad and I went back home that night and me, him, and my mom finished watching a movie as if nothing never happened.

Life can go from perfect to surreal in the matter of minutes. It was years after learning I was adopted that my grandad passed away. This was major for my entire family. This was my next hurdle in my life; accepting this change of losing someone I loved was hard. I can see now that the pain wasn't exactly the fact that I was hurting and missing him. The difficulty was that everyone I loved also lost him and was grieving. I had never experienced the collective grief of a family before. Fortunately, I was also guided through it by my family. Especially my grandma. She has always been a strong woman. Aside from my mother, she is who I admire the most.

When my mom fell ill, I never thought that the last day of my 6th grade year we would be burying her. That was my first year of middle school. I remember being nervous. I didn't want to go to that particular school. But she always lifted me up. She was so sweet and genuine. Not too long after she died, for some reason, my hair started falling out. All of my long, pretty hair seemed to just vanish. And though I always struggled with eczema, my skin became much worse. My dad was trying to do the best he could with me and maintain our life without my mom. We both were. But that is the type of change you're never prepared for and that is the type of hurdle you can never really get over. All you can really do is walk around it, but just like everything I thought I moved past, it stuck with me even years later and it weighed me down.

When we moved in the trailer park I was so spoiled and not humble at all. I look back now wishing I could get those moments back: me and my dad just hanging out at home, leaning on each other more, no matter how much he would curse me out. He was very hard on me. But, I sit and smile at it now because his intentions were good. I love him for making it his job to love me but also to make me strong. During that time, my biological dad found me. Come to find out, he had known nothing about me. I was still kind of young, so mainly I listened to him and my dad talk. Of course, I spoke with him and asked him questions about his life. But, I remember my dad not making me do anything other than that. Sometimes I wish meeting him could have happened much sooner or even just a little bit later because the timing... It was such a bad time. With my grandad and mom passing back to back I didn't have the frame of mind or even the capacity to deal with a newfound parent. I don't want to sound selfish. It's just that I was eleven years old and I really couldn't. I just couldn't care about any of that.

My dad would communicate with my biological family a little but eventually that stopped. Time passed and life went on. The next change in life was my dad being put on dialysis. I started staying with my grandmother. It made it easier for me to be able to catch the bus. He would let me drive myself to school sometimes. It is things like that, that stick with me. Him teaching me how to drive at such a young age and me not knowing at the time it was because he wanted to make sure if there ever was an emergency, I could get him to the hospital.

As I went through high school, struggling with all of the changes since losing my granddad and my mom got easier. I broke more out of the shell I'm not even sure I realized I was hiding behind. I was always honest and true to myself but I used to be very insecure about my skin. That stopped about 10th grade and my skin actually started doing better once I stopped trying to hide it. I got into boys but only a little because I was more of the home girl type after I had watched my older cousins deal with boys. Sometimes they were happy and sometimes not. I watched that closely and I never wanted to feel how it looked like they felt when they were with those guys. So I just stayed away from that for a while. Both my first kiss and first boyfriend happened in the 10th grade. Most of my friends had full blown relationships in middle school but I was chilling, more laid back and just observing.

The older I got, the more I realized I always acted a little older, an "old soul" as some folks would say. I struggled a little managing classes and working my job, but I made it through high school. I made it happen. I went to night school and I walked across the stage on time with my class in 2010. I'll never forget seeing my dad standing tall and stretch his arms out for joy once I crossed that stage. It was something I can never forget. I wish I had more pictures from back then. I never liked to take them much. That's the reason I probably take so many now, for the memories.

Exhale

Imagine holding your breath and not breathing for so long it's as if you've suffocated yourself. That's how it can feel when those old lessons are thrown back at you after you've been pushing them aside and dragging them along with you forever. There just comes a time when your truth wants to arise and you can't smother it any longer. Because you're ready for it and this is the path of your purpose!

As I graduated and attended a community college, my dad and grandmother were both on dialysis, but he was getting sicker. I realized how independent I was, so I decided to get an apartment. My goal was to challenge myself to see if I could pay my own bills and take care of myself in the event something happened to either of them. I got everything together on my own. I looked at different places, I saved money from work and school and I was so excited to tell my dad the day I found the perfect place.

Little did I know that would be the same day he told me he had cancer. At the time I never knew that he had this illness. His death came barely a month later. He never got to see me move in. Those are the things I could only dream of, him helping set up my furniture and getting all of my household needs. Instead, I was planning his funeral the month before I moved in. I was nineteen years old when he passed and for a long time I felt as though I signed his life away when I sent him to hospice. He was only there for about three days and he slept so peacefully. Life works in mysterious ways. That same day, I mentioned to the nurses before I signed that if he was to wake up and wanted to go to dialysis and not be there, I would come remove him myself. That was the same day he died.

I planned to go back to work on that very day. However, as I pulled up in the driveway to get ready, the last picture we took at my aunt's party fell from the visor into my lap. We were standing side by side both smiling so big you could see his gold tooth. I looked at the picture for maybe a minute. Then decided that I wanted to see him again before I went in. I tried to dial my job, but it didn't ring through due to hospice calling me to let me know he passed just about two minutes before that. I remember being very calm and I asked for them not to tell anyone because I would do that. As I went inside and started washing my face, I looked in the mirror and the realization of what the lady had just told me hit me. That was the first time in my life that my breath was completely taken away and I felt as though I was suffocating. I was in shock. My knees went weak and no one was there to pick me up. I had to pick myself up and get myself together. That day I went to the hospice and I sat there with my dad for a while and just talked to him. Of course he was gone, but I needed that time with him. It reminded me of when my mom passed away and we all sat there around her bed. Once everyone walked out, I went back in. I hugged her, kissed her cheek and loved on her for one last moment.

That year in my new apartment was a struggle. I lost my job due to taking days off for my dad. I got other jobs, but they were temporary. I learned how to survive and how to use my money wisely because I had bills to pay. I refused to fail in that apartment. I continued with school up until I had to stop for work reasons. I had to borrow money from time to time. But I always made sure I paid it back and on time, if they even would accept it back. I made the choice to join the military without anyone really knowing. I got to a point where it was best where I did things and then mentioned them after. I didn't say anything about it until right before swearing in and I only told my cousin just so she could know my whereabouts.

Right before I was going to swear in, I got into a really bad accident, running into a light pole and totaling the vehicle completely. I walked away from that with no injuries and a couple tickets I couldn't afford. That situation could have hindered me from going but my faith never wavered. Moving past all of that, I got through basic combat training and then went on to Advance Individual Training (AIT). While in AIT, I got back on my Facebook page to keep in touch with all the new battle buddy's I had met, they are something like your coworkers. I started accepting friend requests not even knowing who some of them were, I then received a long message from someone who I then remembered was my biological dad.

It's funny how I call on my godparents for so much especially my godfather. He is also like my dad in a way because he was my dad's closest friend and brother. He always knows what to say. I explained to him that I'd received a message from my biological dad. I told him how I was good and didn't want to get involved with all of that. I knew once he said, "Darling," it would be something I did not want to hear. But as usual, he was right. He basically explained how it wasn't my father's fault that he didn't know about me and that I should just at least give it a chance. Needless to say, I did, and we've been on a good path for a few years now. There is still a ways to go, but we're getting there. It's kind of weird sometimes knowing I have a different set of family members, including siblings, especially when I never knew they existed. But I have to just take it step by step and day by day.

My last journey overseas was right after my biggest heartbreak in a different way. This was more of a love pain. I didn't realize I had guarded my heart so much to the point where I couldn't even handle certain situations. I mean, how can you know how to deal with some relationship issues if you haven't allowed yourself to really be with someone? Don't get me wrong, I've loved and been loved back. But this was different. I was older. I wanted more. I wanted a future not a "just because" type relationship. His spirit was so welcoming, his consistency, personality and even honesty was what drew me in to just say "Fu*k it, why not!" I felt comfortable with him, I met his family and although my relationship with them grew after our breakup, it was always genuine.

See, the way things align also means a lot to me. We didn't work as a couple at that moment, but I learned a lot from him, and I learned even more about him afterwards. I still had to give myself time to heal. For a while, I tried to think about what I could have done differently. My intentions were never bad and I certainly never wanted to invade his space. But I was confused by some of his actions. I just needed to be reassured that we were good. It took time for me to realize I couldn't fully blame myself because I wasn't solely in the wrong, but I did have to also take time and give myself an overview. I know what I could have done just a little different. I figured out how I could have handled or reacted to our situation, and I examined some of the reasons why his communication just shut down at times without warning.

It wasn't all me, it was some of him too. If I could go back, I wouldn't change things even though I realized some stuff I could fix about me. I would let it happen how it's supposed to, how it was destined to, and learn from it exactly how I did. For that I thank him. Past the hurt and the heartache, I appreciate him for helping me to discover that missing piece to my life's puzzle. I would have hated to be in my mid-thirties and just now figuring out some of my ways in a relationship setting. Overall it, was a great experience and I still think about the "what if's" at times, but life goes on and only time will tell.

I Am Strength

"How does it feel?"

That is the question that I get asked the most. This is such an open-ended question for me, so I need more specifics. I have to ask in return, "How does what feel?" because there are so many things that fit into the "it" of their question. The answers vary.

"Being adopted? Losing the two people who raised you, loved you, and taught you to be the woman you are today? Being a part of so many families? Trying to be able to self-heal? Or, opening your heart and mind to want to interact with or even be a part of your biological side?"

No matter what the specific question is, I have to take a breath and remember to answer honestly, no matter how hard it might be. As you may have guessed by now, my story is no longer for me. It's for you and so many others. I'm realizing that answering these painful and personal questions honestly are all a part of the process. Learning about my adoption was surreal for me. Coming from one set of parents and being adopted into a family that loved me one hundred percent as one of their own, and then having godparents whose family accepts me is the greatest gift and blessing any child can have. It did feel as if there was a war inside of me. One side wanting to be loyal to the parents that loved and raised me. The other side needing to know more about the parents that made me. But it was my dad that ended this war for me. As he lie in bed, sick with cancer, he and my biological father conversed. What they discussed I'm not quite sure, but I know that my father wouldn't feel betrayed or threatened by my need to know where I came from. Even though there was so much that transpired leading up to these moments.

I have to admit that I never had a desire to meet my biological mother. I knew certain things about her, of course. But for the most part she was like a ghost and I chose not to even entertain the thought of trying to have her replace the mother that raised me. But, there was one small question that I did want to know. No one could tell me for certain what time I was born. You see, my birth certificate was delayed due to me being born at home and given directly to my parents, as far as I know. As a matter of fact, I didn't get an official copy of my birth certificate until I graduated from high school. It was a court-ordered birth certificate, and I'm sure it must seem like a small thing to most people, but it was exciting seeing my name on paper encased in the language of "Being born on this date... to Mother... and Father..." I was so happy to finally have it, the record of my birth, an official record and information that I can pass on my children, if I ever have any.

Being born at home and not having an official birth certificate until I became an adult may seem like a story from olden times and yes, my adoption was like something out of a movie. My biological mother hid her pregnancy from everyone. I cannot tell you why the secrecy was so important to her and I won't try to figure it out either. So, I was born at home and passed to a woman out of a window. This woman took me to my parents. I've never looked at this as if it was something negative. I never knew her situation so I couldn't judge her. Yes, I've had some thoughts toward her that were less than kind, because I'm human. But, I see that she cared enough to put me with a good man and woman. Also, what an incredible sacrifice it must have been for her to choose not to terminate her pregnancy and give me life.

Years have passed since that day under the window, and I'm twenty-six years old now. For all of the information the birth certificate gave me, I still didn't know the time of my birth. After joking about this one evening on the phone with my aunt, we decided to find my biological mother's brother and I politely messaged him. A few days later, he responded with her information and his. Once I had it, I couldn't wait. I instantly gave her a call and just began asking questions. Talking with her was like an end to a mystery and I could feel the beginning of something new. I even stated I would try to meet up with her the next time I was in town. We ended up meeting and I got to hear her side of the story. Whether or not she was right or wrong, and no matter what she said, it would never change my feelings for my parents. I sometimes wish they were here so I could ask them the questions I should have while they were still with me. Just certain things. But, I have to take it for what it is and keep moving forward.

To my surprise, my biological mother knew a lot about me. She had been watching me for a while. It was important to her even though she could not keep and take care of me, that she make sure I was doing well. I took the time to learn somethings about her and her family. I'm not perfect and I've never claimed to be. My life is a lot to take in sometimes. However, I've managed to do so and look now I can see everything that has happened and everything that I have been through as God's triumphant plan for my life.

My biological mother and I touch base with each other sometimes. I'm sure with time it will get better between us. I can hear it in her voice that she is really excited to hear from and talk to me. I do understand some of her reasons for giving me up for adoption, being a young adult without many options or much guidance. I could never allow anyone to fill my head up with anything negative about her after our meeting. For what? It's pointless and that was almost thirty years ago. My whole life I dreamed of being on a television show. I loved television and watching movies and all along I was starring in a film called My Life.

Having multiple families that love me and treat me like nothing other than their own is a true blessing. I am humbled each time they express to me that they feel I was the blessing to them. My parents were amazing despite their life challenges. They got me through school the best way they could. My dad used his street knowledge in everything he taught me so the streets wouldn't be able to teach me anything that he already hadn't. My mom was so sweet and pure with a heart of raw gold, embedding her loving and caring spirit upon me, as well as her drive to give and be genuine. My grandmother is the strongest lady I know. She placed her spiritual knowledge and guidance around my life from day one. My uncles and aunts are a bit talkative sometimes, but real. They are also messy at times, but loving. I can't live with them and can't live without them. My god-siblings are nothing less than my brothers and sisters. The players on the team my dad coached while I was coming up became a life-long family, and they won't miss a beat when it comes to me.

There is so much to my story and I'm so thankful I didn't let anything break me. I searched deep and relived through it all to appreciate and embrace it. A part of me was resting inside while I was channeling other pieces of me. Even when I looked back and couldn't understand everything, I've learned to accept it and move on. The things I've written about in this book were based on different parts of me, my life, my story. The places I see my future going and the vision over my life.

This is my life's prayer:

"*Jehovah God, I come to you thanking you for all you have done for me, my family, friends and loved ones. I ask you to forgive me for my debts as I forgive my debtors. I pray not to dis love something I have a passion for that you have placed upon my life's footprint, I pray to remain focused in all that I do, to be guided, forgiven for my short comings, remain humble and thankful, to be strengthened spiritually, mentally and physically for myself, my family and others. To be placed in a position to place others in a better position. To be able to speak wisdom, knowledge and life unto others. I am still a work in progress, and I ask for you to continue to teach and show me the truths of my life so I can share it with those surrounding me. I pray upon my business for expansion, good health in my family, for friends near and far to be spiritually strong, touched by you and keep faith. I ask that I receive more of you than me. Jehovah, I thank you for all the lessons. Lastly God, expose me to my destiny and legacy. I pray to you for all these things in your son Jesus Christ name, Amen.*

To God and all of His Glory, how Fortunate am I, my life was a Miracle, to meet someone that opened my mind to evaluate myself without them even knowing they taught me a lesson was a part of my Destiny. I've grown overtime to learn to have Patience, while God granted me the Serenity I needed to keep my Faith strong. Most say Genesis is the beginning, the mode of forming something, and that may be so, but this shift, this weight, this life is my New Beginning. Accepting, forgiving, learning and regaining is a part of my new beginning. As I sit here and realize I have excelled to the next phase of my life and will no longer suffocate my truth. I've let so much of my life out in a matter of pages. I sit here with my fingers flowing so freely across the keyboard to finally say, "I have Exhaled".

My name is Jaira B. Williams and I AM STRENGTH.

ABOUT THE AUTHOR

Influencer, Inspiration Pusher, and CEO of Pretty Mink'd Out Beauty Collection, Jaira B. Williams is a leader in her own right. A graduate of Central Texas College, she successfully serves as an Active Duty Noncommissioned Officer in the United States Army. Her life story has truly been one of strength. Growing up in a loving family, Jaira B. would have never envisioned the lessons placed upon her life's path. She has learned to relive her truth, accept it and share it with the purpose for others to understand the power in self-love, self-help, and acknowledging things that life causes us to ignore.

Jaira B. has overcome many obstacles that could have broken her, but she is the epitome of being not easily broken. Believing that God makes no mistakes, she has learned to own her purpose and aims to encourage others to own theirs. To experience more of what Jaira B. Williams purveys visit:

Her website: www.prettyminkdout.com

Facebook Page: Jaira Williams

Instagram: Iamjairab

WHAT'S YOUR STORY OF STRENGTH?

Start My Process Here:

ACCEPT WHAT YOU'VE IGNORED!

What can I acknowledge that I've ignored?

_____

_____

_____

_____

_____

_____

_____

_____

_____

_____

_____

_____

_____

_____

_____

_____

_____

_____

Quiet Your Mind & Let Your Soul Speak!

Relaxation is KEY! Just WRITE IT!

_____

_____

_____

_____

_____

_____

_____

_____

_____

_____

_____

_____

_____

_____

_____

_____

_____

_____

_____

_____

Strengths vs. Challenges

My Strengths Come
From?

My Challenges Are?

_____
_____
_____
_____
_____
_____
_____
_____
_____
_____
_____
_____
_____
_____
_____
_____
_____
_____

Master-PEACE!

What gives me Peace?
What Calms my Spirit?
What makes me feel FREE!

_____

_____

_____

_____

_____

_____

_____

_____

_____

_____

_____

_____

_____

_____

_____

_____

_____

_____

_____

Becoming Me!

How I Aspire to Become a Better Me

_____

_____

_____

_____

_____

_____

_____

_____

_____

_____

_____

_____

_____

_____

_____

_____

_____

_____

_____

_____

It's Never Too Late!

What are the Steps to Making My Visions Visible?

_____

_____

_____

_____

_____

_____

_____

_____

_____

_____

_____

_____

_____

_____

_____

_____

_____

_____

My Goals

_____

_____

_____

_____

_____

_____

_____

_____

_____

_____

_____

_____

_____

_____

_____

_____

_____

_____

_____

_____

_____

_____

_____

_____

_____

_____

✓ Accepting What I've Ignored
✓ Mind Relaxation & Mediation
✓ Letting My Strengths WIN!
✓ I've Mastered My Peace
✓ Motivation, Dedication & Consistency
✓ Becoming a Better Me
✓ Making My Visions Visible
✓ My GOALS

Get Ready, Get Set...
My Shift, My Power, My New
Beginning Starts NOW!!

I'm Most Proud of Myself For...

_____

_____

_____

_____

_____

_____

_____

_____

Owning Your Purpose

Stepping into your purpose with confidence is not only of value to you. Use that to inspire and influence others. Take a leap out of your comfort zone TODAY! Put action behind your dreams. The process starts with YOU! Seek Guidance, Faith, Determination, and let God be your Source.

Made in the
USA
Middletown, DE